A Memoir
by Ms. Fifi Frost

Rusted
Rhinestones

RUSTED RHINESTONES

MS. FIFI FROST

(Edit by Barbi Winterhalder and Fifi Frost)
(Image Design by Barbi & John Winterhalder)

Copyright 2015 by Ms. Fifi Frost

Table of Contents

Chapter 1

As I sit to write, I am faced with memories. Some good some bad, fear, but mostly pride that I have made it this far. My story is true, there are ups, downs, tears, laughter and pain. Yes and love, lots of love from many I would learn to call family. Not from my blood but from my heart.

My earliest memories come from a very small town in Louisiana named Jigger. I have to have been 3 or 4 years old because we moved to Monroe Louisiana right before my fifth birthday. I am the youngest, there is my older brother David, and Mom and Dad. The house was old, it belonged to my grandmother, on my mother's side of the family. I have vague memories of visiting her in a nursing home. Asking to please let her hold little David's and little James's hands. She was a diabetic and had lost her eyesight and part of her leg. I remember she did not live very long after the surgery. Dave and I had a very happy start in life, or so I thought. There were cotton fields outside the back door of the house, the road was gravel and I remember us spending many hours of the day just playing. We always had pets and the first I remember were two kittens. Dave named his 5 and I am sure that had to have been his age, I named mine Green. I would like to think at the time green was my favorite color. There were always baby rabbits coming out of the fields and I remember them being easy to catch, along with baby opossums. Can't tell you how many of those we raised, well, until mom or dad saw us not looking and set them free. Another fond memory, we had an old washing machine on the front porch. With the rollers on top and a gasoline engine. When mom used it, she would fill it up with the garden hose and there was a black pipe that went from the tub of the washer then across the porch and down to the ground. When she was finished and let the water out, David and I would run to the end of the pipe. It was wet, smelled good and made mud! The best substance on the planet. Dave would play with his trucks as I made and decorated mud pies. She would hang the laundry out to dry in the back yard on a line that seemed to stretch forever. I loved the smell of my clothes from drying in the sun.

Mom was a stay at home housewife and dad owned a cotton picker along with these huge trailers. He would plant cotton on our land and also picked cotton for others in the area. Dad would drive the picker down the rows and once the basket on back was full he would go to one of those trailers and dump the basket. As soon as he was away from the trailer David and I would climb up and in to stomp the cotton. Really to compress it so the trailer would hold more. Mom was there to help too because we didn't weigh very much at the time. As we grew I remember David going off to kindergarten and there would just be mom and me at home during the day. Mom had her ways, you didn't bother her, nor did you wake her if she was napping. I would do my best to keep quiet, but, there were times I wasn't very successful. Let's just say she wasn't happy being disturbed. The first thing she could get her hands on is what you got hit with. A hairbrush, coffee cup, book, you get the idea. I remember a store in Wisner Louisiana, my Aunt worked there, dad's sister. He came from a family of 9 children. She always hugged us so tight when we would visit. You will read more about her later, she was a very good friend to me. As kids do we went straight to the aisle where the toys were. David to a baseball glove, me to a plastic tea set. Oh it was so pretty, white with multi colored flowers in it. I picked it up as to get a better look, when mom saw me she yelled put it down and then in front of everyone slapped me across my face. I saw stars. Then she said loudly, James thinks he is a little girl. I was so embarrassed. Everyone in the store was laughing, except my aunt. Then mom said stop crying you little sissy or I will give you something to cry about. Even at that young age I knew I was different than my brother, I just didn't know why. Dad was not as strict, but, he was away from home working most of the time. I remember them arguing nonstop, it seemed to never end. Mom liked her beer and whiskey. Dad would ever so often have a beer, but, it was rare. One day the parents took us to our aunt's house. They had put some of our clothes in a paper grocery bag. We were excited because that meant we were spending the night. She had 3 kids herself and we loved our cousins. I still remember the smell of the chicken she was frying for dinner. At the time mom and dad were house hunting, but we didn't know it. After we played, ate and finished with our baths we helped pull out the sofa bed. My aunt asked me. Does your mom hit you boys like that all the time? I answered only when we are bad. She said you two are never bad. I think back, she was right. But at the time I didn't know any better.

David had a speech problem and I had noticed he was not like me or any of our cousins. He was withdrawn, not good with his homework and seemed to me he just wanted to be in his room with his stuff. He didn't like anyone touching his belongings and everything had its place. I learned early on not to touch his toys when we were playing. It seemed our parents were always yelling at him and he stayed in trouble. When dad was gone mom would whip David with a switch or a belt. She was very heavy handed with both of us when it came to discipline. It seemed he could not do anything right in their eyes, so I did my best to just please them. I didn't want to be whipped all the time. With David's speech sometimes the parents would look at me so I could translate what he had said. I didn't mind, honestly I could understand everything he said, I wondered why they couldn't. More on that later.

Every summer of our youth David and I went to Mississippi so we could stay with another aunt and her family. Mom's only sister, her husband and they had two girls. We loved it. Not one time in all those years did we ever get in trouble while we were there. Mom and dad would drive us over, spend the weekend and then come back for us in 14 days. This side of the family all liked to drink alcohol. When they got together they did, PLENTY! Dad and his family didn't so it was fun for us to see them being silly. But, the silly never lasted. It usually ended up in a big ole fight. Being children we didn't know any better so we thought this was how all families were. Mom's family and dad's never did anything together. I found out later in life they thought he had married beneath himself. We would from time to time visit some of dad's family, but, not often. There are many David and I have never met. If mom could get away we always went to her sisters in Mississippi. She seemed happier being away from dad, so we saw this part of the family several times a year.

One evening I remember it being cold outside, there was some ice on the ground as we walked to the car. Mom said we were going to look at something in Monroe. It was only about 30 miles, but to a kid it felt like cross country. Where we lived in Jigger I could not see a neighbor's house in the summer and in winter with no leaves on the trees we could see one with the lights on in the distance. We drove into town, well to us a big city and then turn on a street by a service station. We drive a few blocks, I ask dad why the houses are so close together? He said in the city there was not as much room and they had to build this way. I said ok, but, still thought it was dumb. The car slows down, then we stop. Mom asked us. Y'all see that gray house? Yes ma'am. Well it is ours, we will be moving soon. I remember thinking as we drove away, how and where would dad plant and pick cotton? Where would we put the trailers to stomp in? Mom had two brothers as well as her sister and they all showed up on moving day. The kids had one job, stay the hell out of the grown up's way. Dad brought one of the empty cotton trailers, had the back open and they started to load it up. It was still a little chilly, but, spring was coming. Everyone was laughing, talking and I remember Hank Williams Sr. on the record player. The adult beverages flowed like water. I can only imagine what the neighbors thought as we caravanned down the street to the new house. Two cars full of kids, three pickup trucks, with one pulling this huge trailer. Dad managed to get the trailer backed up to the carport and the first thing mom unpacked was the record player as my aunt stocked the fridge with food and the coolers with beer. Johnny Horton in the background marching to The Mighty Mississippi! The house had 3 bedrooms, one bathroom, kitchen, dining and living room. There was a utility room and we were thrilled to see a washer and dryer in it. Mom had painted the cabinet's granny smith apple green and made curtains to match. The stove was gas, we had to strike a match to light the burners. Even the oven, we would drop a lit match in this little hole after we turned on the gas for a few seconds. Looking back it is a wonder we didn't blow the entire house up. With the small army of relatives the unpacking was quick. I remember when all was done, them sitting around the dining table, one with a guitar and dad with his harmonica as everyone sang Lovesick Blues and North to Alaska. The youngest of the girls was only a few months older than David, she had some plastic high heel shoes that had come in a dress up set from the dollar store. They were clear and had gold glitter. I wanted those BAD! While the adults were at the table and the others watching the television in the living room, I snuck off to try them on. Oh how good I looked in them. About 2 inches high and I was walking like a pro. That is until one of the heels broke off. A problem I would unfortunately have again later in life. Well I had to see if I could fix them. I took some Elmer's glue and did my best. It didn't hold so I took them to dad and asked if he could fix them for me. Mom saw them, took me by my arm and we were off to the bathroom. I don't remember how many times she hit me, but, I was bruised from head to toe. She made me apologize to my cousin for breaking them. Her reply was, they are not for boys!! I still laugh at that to this day.

Chapter 2

David and I were sharing a bedroom in the new house. It was smaller than the old one but much nicer. It was, as I learned from dad, on a slab. He said we would not have the pipes freeze like in the old house. So no waiting to flush the toilet in the winter. We had shag carpet and central heat. The window air conditioning units came later. The settling in was uneventful and soon it was time to register for school. I was 5, pumped and ready for kindergarten. Turned out with my birthday being in December I was headed straight to first grade. That was fine with me, I had it all figured out. I thought one day in school was for one grade. So by the end of the week I would be in fifth grade. I would be out of high school in a few more weeks and, was ready to take on the world. Sadly that wasn't how it worked.

We liked our neighbors, I was making friends at school, so it looked like things were going to be ok. I was a tiny kid. Didn't hit a good growth spurt until around seventh grade. Seemed like I grew a foot that summer, but, I am getting ahead of myself.

I would say it was third grade when the kids at school started to notice I wasn't like the other boys. I played four square, jump rope and was the best jacks' player in the southern hemisphere. All of my friends were girls and one I still know today. She is my insurance lady, she also is the one so many years ago that taught me to tie my shoes. A skill I can finally say I have mastered. The boys started to pick on me some. I didn't really mind the nicknames, because I had no idea what they were talking about. I would just laugh, or say thank you and go on my way. I passed David in third grade, was a good student, but still knew I was different. They started to socially promote David after that so he would not get too far behind the kids he started school with. This turned out to be the path of us finding out about his Autism.

Mom was very hard on David. I did not like her always comparing him to me and his abuse really escalated when I passed him in school. I was so scared she was going to turn on me one day too. For the time being she would give me ice cream and toys for making good grades, but, not my brother. That hurt him, I look back and wish I could change so much, but, we can't.

It had gotten to where dad was gone for months at a time. He had been in the military as a young man, Korean War and had learned to weld. He bought a work truck, welder and went on the road. He must have been good at it because we always had food, clothes and mom spent like crazy.

I believe I was six years old when mom said we were going to visit a church she was interested in. So she woke us up one Saturday morning to get dressed. This was usually time spent eating cereal and watching cartoons. I thought to myself church on Saturday? The place is a rented building, folded metal chairs and smelled like a skunk farted. So we sit, stand, sing. Sit, stand, sing like church aerobics. David and I both got the dreaded thump on the head for falling asleep. But, all in all everyone seemed to be nice enough. We sat quietly with mom and the pastor as they talked. When she had finished her questions it was time to go. Dad was coming home that night so as soon as we arrived home, mom mixed a drink. She told us to clean the house, as she chained smoked Winston 100's and sipped Southern Comfort mixed with Mountain Dew. She had already started her decline into mental illness then, but, as a kid I did not see it. Dad was late getting in so mom was TANKED when he walked through the door. I remember he brought us a small transistor radio each. We were on cloud nine and, that was the boom box of the 1970's. Both had horrible sound, all treble, the antenna pulled out it seemed seven feet and they stopped working the first time we dropped them. So the parents start in on each other right off the bat. It was bed time for us boys, so we left them the front of the house to fight in. I don't remember what time it was when mom came into the room to wake me. She told me to go to her friend's house, two doors down. Ring the doorbell and have them call the police, that dad had beaten her up. Looking back, we had a phone. I learned at an early age, adults who drank in excess, did not make since most of the time. Now mom was five foot eleven, dad, on tip toe would have been five foot six, but I did as she told me. The neighbor kept me with her until the police arrived. Then she walked me back. Dave is up and crying, mom had whipped him, parent of the year was in the bathroom throwing up, dad says to the policeman I just can't handle her anymore. Turns out he had put her over his knee and gave her a spanking. Which some enjoy I hear. Rest assured she didn't.

The police take mom, to what dad called, the nut house. When it was time for dad to leave, so he could go back to work, he asked the neighbor to look after us. Back then we lived in a safer world. It was not unusual for people to leave the kids with friends or family. I remember the afternoon we came in from school and mom was home. She was not a happy camper and something about her had changed. She was hateful, more abusive than ever and when I looked into her eyes, no one was looking back. I learned a new term. Nerve Pills. Better known as Valium. Her drinking really increased as well as her smoking. It was three blocks to the service station at the end of our street, so rain or shine, she would send me walking, or on my bike to buy her cigarettes. Back then they sold to anyone! So this preacher from our church comes over for a visit. This time he wanted to see mom and dad. He tells them they have to divorce, because the church doesn't believe in second marriages. I thought WHAT THE HELL? Turns out mom was married for like eight days a few years before she met dad. I still don't know all the details on that. Later in life I did ask mom's sister about this man. All she would say was that he was very mean to my mom and that she was very happy she got away from him. For many months the thought of divorce weighed heavily on mom, she took all of her frustrations out on David and me. Final decision from the church was they didn't have to divorce after all, the church changed its rules after it came out the pastor's son was on his third.

I have often wondered if they had divorced, how our lives would have changed. So now we are full members of the Worldwide Church of God. The pastor had to come to the house, he and several deacons had to anoint us with oil, bless the house and even bless out clothes to stop a demon from getting us. See we were God's chosen people and we were targets for the devil. We had to give up birthdays, Christmas, Easter, Halloween and in return we inherited all of these Holy Days. Which by the way none of them had anything to do with gifts or cake! No pork, no shell fish and by no pork they meant bacon too! Mom and dad had to start counseling with this man, also they hosted and went to home bible studies with other members. This is about the time when spare the rod, spoil the child talks started. For David and me, things were about to get much worse.   As we were making the adjustments to our new church, things at school for me were going downhill fast. We couldn't celebrate Valentine's Day, Birthdays and Christmas so the weird kid just became weirder. I remember classmates giving me a card or gift, me having to say I can't have it. I was embarrassed and it hurt that I was not included in the festivities. As the other kids did reports on Christmas, I had to do mine on why I didn't believe in it. I always got an F and my teachers were not impressed at all. Most of my classmates resented me for not being a part of the group. For me it was a very tough situation to be put in.

By now David had been moved to special education classes, to me he just seemed to have shut down. As I think back, I know he had to have had issues with bullies too, but, David pretty much just beat up anyone who crossed him. He knew he would be paddled at school and beat for it when he got home. He always stood up for himself on the playground. And David was becoming a very big boy.

Our school was first through ninth grade, so there were older teens as well. They turned out to be the worst of them all for me. The fag and cocksucker comments started. Pushing me into lockers. Dunking my head in the toilet after several took a shit in it. The rite of passage that so many call that time in life. In the beginning of my 7th grade year, I had some older teens hold me in the locker room after everyone had gone outside. They would hold me down and rub their crotches in my face. Their gym clothes stunk. There was one who would pull me into the equipment room. He would make me open my mouth, then he would put in his erect penis. I was so scared. This abuse went on for the rest of the year. On two occasions one or our coaches saw this happening to me. He did absolutely nothing to stop it, or help me. He just walked away both times. To this day I wonder why he didn't help. I see the man who did this to me from time to time on the streets, I do not speak.

Chapter 3

As I had said earlier, we always had pets. We learned a very valuable lesson about boy dogs and chain link fences. Prissy, mom's poodle was in heat. The back yard was fenced so no one worried about her for the few minutes she needed to go out and do her business. Well there are some clever dogs out there, so clever that one in particular could climb a five foot fence. I hear mom yell for dad to get the water hose that Prissy was mating with a mutt. Well he was a smart mutt because he was finished and climbing the fence to leave as dad ran out the back door. We all laughed as he ran away. So Prissy has puppies. We gave 2 away and they let us keep one each, as long as we promised to take care of them and they were to be outside dogs. David named his Brownie, he was brown. I named mine Nubbin because he was born with a bob tail. He was blonde and I just loved him. It did us good to go to the back yard and play with them.

The preacher gave mom a book he wanted us to read. God speaks on the "New Morality". So we agree, but, honestly we are not interested, it had no pictures. I didn't even know what he thought about the old morality. I didn't know what morality was.

I hadn't said anything about being bullied, the things from PE class, or that even some of my teachers had started making comments about me in class. One teacher I had for math could not stand me. He had to be one of the nastiest persons I have ever met in my life. During his math class he would call on me as Sissy, or Jamie Swift. What a complete asshole he was to me.

So we are trying to survive our home and school life. One night, I remember it was winter. There was an ice storm. Dad was not able to get home as he planned because of the weather. Mom was taking her nerve pills, drinking and smoking. All the housework and cooking had fallen to me by the time I was in fifth grade. David had all yard and flower gardens to tend. He would also help me in the house. Anyway, we were watching TV, one of the three channels we got back then and after dad called mom just went off. Told us her life was perfect until she had kids and how we had ruined her and her marriage. All I said was I am sorry mom. She grabbed me and just started punching me with closed fists. Mom was 5 ft. 11 and now about 230 pounds. She let me go, grabbed David, doing the same to him. I was screaming at her to stop, so she grabbed the broom, then started hitting us with the wooden handle. She threw down the broom, made us take off all of our clothes, except for our underwear. Then sent us outside in an ice storm to sleep. David asked me what he had done to make her so mad. I told him he had not done anything, then he said I am sorry I got you in trouble. About an hour later she called for us to come back into the house, Hit us a few more times, then sent us to bed. By Monday the ice was clearing and we were headed to school. Most everything was covered up by our jeans and long sleeve shirts. I only had one teacher ask about the large bruise on my face. I said I had fallen down on the ice, just what mom told me to say. This was the first of many severe beatings to come.

Mom would get a call from dad on the road and instantly go into a rage. We had no way to defend ourselves against her. Her eyes would be blank inside. Sometimes after she was finished beating on us, she would get us to sit beside her on the sofa, one on either side. She would rock back and forth and cry. Now the people in our church started to notice I was a fem boy, a sissy, some wouldn't even let their children play with me. Dad was never in town so he had no idea how these people were. We had guest pastors come in to give special sermons from time to time. This one Saturday was to change my life forever. Turns out mom had already asked our pastor about me and if he thought I might be possessed by a demon. If anyone was it was Ms. Nerve Pill and not me. This begins the journey that would eventually send me to Anti-Gay Conversion Therapy. Or as I call it, Rape Camp.

Now I was still getting good grades at school, even if I was catching hell, it wasn't as bad as being home. I was getting punched and called names daily now at home and school.

I believe it was a Tuesday morning English class when I first saw him. Buzz cut dark hair and the greenest eyes I had ever seen. The haircut was odd because it was the late 70's and we all were doing our best to grow our hair and be either Starsky or Hutch. He seemed to be quiet, but, there was just something about him. I know I must have stared at him the entire class. I knew every curve of his profile and every small scar on the back of his head. When it was time for lunch, I made sure I sat as close to him as possible, but, not to bring attention to myself. I was building up my courage to speak. The cool kids started talking with him so I figured he would probably be the next one to call me a name, push me down, or even worse. The others walked away and he stayed seated. "Hi my name is James, are you new here?" Oh I thought to myself, STUPID, STUPID, yes it was his first day dumbass! I wanted to crawl under a rock. He introduced himself, we started to talk. He wasn't in band, didn't want to play on any of the sports teams and for some reason he just made my heart beat like crazy. As the weeks went by we became friends, I didn't care about anything else in my life. I just wanted to be near him. I will call him C.K. My being bullied did slack up some. I think because I wasn't doing everything by myself anymore.

The other students would talk about sleepovers, or weekends at each other's houses. C.K. asked me to come over for a cookout, I couldn't. I knew not to even ask mom. David and I were not allowed to have company over, mom was just against it, plus I didn't want anyone to see how she acted anyway. She had really started to close herself off from people by that time.

One thing that developed in me very early was my love of music. Mom had her records and eight track tapes. She would put on Ace Cannon, or Boots Randolph and we would just dance all around the living room. So in sixth grade when it was time to sign up for band I begged them to be able to. They said yes and I was going to learn how to play the Saxophone. Thinking back those were my happiest memories of being in school. I fit in with this group and was very good playing my sax. I kept first chair most of my time in this band. Mom and dad never came to my concerts, nor to any of David's football games. She would just drop us off and then pick us up when we finished. That is if she let us go at all. I lost a solo once because she refused to take me to the concert. My band director was furious at me. So back to C.K. We had a band party planned, I asked mom if I could go. She said I could once I finished my chores, which should have been hers by the way. The next day at school I asked C.K. if he wanted to come to the party. He said he didn't care about the party, but, would like to spend some time with me. Was music to my ears, we decided to meet and just ditch the party all together. Mom would drop me off, I had two hours, then she would come back to get me. I know I tried on every shirt I owned until I found the right one. Mom dropped me off and drove away. I walked around to the back of the band room and there he was. I could have been shot dead on the spot and I would not have cared. This time we were able to talk without anyone else listening. I asked him why he was so nice to me when everyone else called me a fag. I now knew what that word meant. He asked me, well are you one? I didn't know what to say, honestly I didn't know myself. I had so much shit in my life all I was trying to do was just get through the day. At first I said no, not at all. I was worried I was about to get my ass kicked. He said that's a shame, because I am. I ask you are one what? He said a fag. I think I peed a little. I answered I may be one, that I just didn't know. He asked, do you want to find out? Before I could even answer he took his hand, gently pulled my face to his and kissed me. Not a peck, a real kiss. Like I had seen in Gone with the Wind! At that second I had no question what I was. I was and, honey I was a big one! He was so gentle, his lips were so soft. I melted inside. We didn't kiss again for 2 weeks. I had found someone who was like me. It was like blinders being taken off for the very first time, I could see the sun and all of the beauty in the world. Having his arms around me, for the first time in my life I felt safe. Thinking back, if we would have been caught making out, well the outcome would not have been good. That was the fastest two hours of my life. Mom drove up and I went home.

The next weekend mom asked if I had read the morality book yet. I answered no ma'am. She kicked me in the shin so hard I thought my leg was broken. I did get quite a dent in my bone. This was Friday night. I had it read cover to cover by Saturday afternoon. In the book there was one small section about homosexuality. Just a few paragraphs. I took the book to mom, told her I identified more with this small section than any other part of the book. She must have blacked out for a second, because she hit me with an open hand instead of a closed fist. This would turn out to be the worst beating she would ever give me. I missed 2 weeks of school. She came into my room, David and I now had separate rooms, sat on my bed and told me. Every night your father is not here you will be sleeping with me. I wasn't happy about it but, there was nothing I could do. As if our mother, son relationship was not strained enough with her constant booze, pill popping abuse, that night after we went to bed. This is very hard for me to type. She said you must respond to a woman's touch. With that she started molesting me and I honestly don't think I will ever get over it. I prayed to God, please kill me. PLEASE KILL ME.

Chapter 4

Mom was thinking about going to beauty school, I had no idea why, but in time it would all be clear. We went to church that Saturday, after the service mom told the pastor what I had said about the book. He sat me down as they went into his office to talk. I just sat there, wondering what was coming next. After what seemed an eternity they came back to me. The pastor asked me. Do you want to go to hell? I answered no sir. He asked do you want your family to go to hell because of you. Again I answered no sir. He looked at mom and said, all four of your souls are in jeopardy, you have got to get him right with God. He looked at me and said, I can only imagine the disgust your parents have for you. Because I can't stand the very sight of you.

So we get in the car and go home. I had a yellow parakeet named of all things Tweety, her cage was in the corner of the dining room near a built in bookshelf. I tended to her and kept her cage clean as were the rules for me to have her. Mom told me to go to my room and she would be in later. I figured I was about to get the crap beat out of me so I just sat on my bed. Hoping she would come on and get it over with. Awhile later mom came into my room. She had my bird in one hand, my dog Nubbin on his leash and a pair of scissors in her other hand. She told me to close the door. I did. Right in front of me she took the scissors and cut my birds head off, dropped her body on the floor. I was in shock, I could not believe what I had just seen. Then she took the scissors and started stabbing Nubbin in the throat, he screamed and then he was quiet. I wanted to scream but, I couldn't. Their blood was everywhere. She opened my door then told me to clean it up. I told her I was going to throw up. She said wait here, she came back with a small glass with some whiskey in it. She cracked an egg, dropped it in the glass. Said drink it fast and that I had better not set sick. Well it came up faster than it went down and I threw up all over her. The whiskey took my breath away. She punched me in the face and said clean your mess up now. MY MESS? I have to be honest with you. I have only talked about this with very few people in my life. C.K. my cousin and Boo. If I tend to stray it is only a defense mechanism. I have spent my entire life trying to forget all of this, but, I just can't. I take a plastic lawn and leaf bag, I place Tweety and Nubbin as gently as I could in it. Then I take the bag outside to the barrel dad burns some trash in. So while I was trying to clean my floor, I hear David scream. Mom I will behave I promise. Then he screamed in pain. I ran to his room to see if she still had the scissors, thankfully she only hit and bit him. We were just the shell of children, we had died inside. The daily cycle for me was abuse at school, abuse at home, it was more than I could bare. I found it odd my father never asked me where my bird and dog were.

The church said if you had to punish one of your children for doing something wrong, you had to punish all of them even if they had not done anything. Mom would walk by us, hit, slap, or kick us. She would say I know one of you will do something later to deserve this. One time I did get in trouble for dropping a glass unloading the dishwasher, she had hurt my hand the day before. So she slapped me. I said you already hit me earlier for nothing remember? That was not my brightest moment I can assure you.

Going back to school I was at least looking forward to seeing C.K. I did tell him some of what was going on at my house, but, it was many years later when I told him everything, Once again I am getting ahead of myself.

So we fast forward to the summer. C.K. called me, his father was being transferred, they were moving in just a few weeks. All we had were brief telephone conversations, he knew my mom listened in on every call. I was devastated inside and could not show one emotion. We had a new pastor coming to our church, they changed them up every few years, for what reason I do not know. Mom had the old one over to the house with some people for one last visit. I didn't know them and I only recognized the pastor and one man who had given a sermon a few years back. Dad came home for this meeting. This was when I learned I was going away to camp after I turned 15. I was so excited because I had heard others in my school talk about their summer camp fun. Swimming, cooking and taking hikes. I wanted to leave then. Boy was I wrong.

David was having tooth problems, mom refused to take him to the dentist. She had the new pastor come by, anoint him with oil, say a prayer, then he left. She then took David to the kitchen and had him lay on his back. She sat on his chest with her knees over his arms. She had me help hold him in place as she tied thread around his teeth one at a time, then would yank the thread. I know we were there at least three hours with him screaming, begging her to stop. She would hit him, I was crying and the occasional slap across my face to remind me to shut up. It was horrible and I will never be able to forgive myself for helping to hold him down. He says he has forgotten about it that I had no choice and it was all mom anyway. This will shed some light on why I am so devoted to my brother. I know the abuse he suffered from her hands. After that day I knew I had to do something.

The parents sat us down one afternoon after school, dad had a talk with us about doing more around the house and the yard because mom was going to beauty school. She didn't clean the house or work in the yard, we did. Dad didn't know that. Dad asked David why he was wearing a long sleeve shirt and jeans. It was summer, we had the air on. Mom slapped me across my face, said because James didn't do the laundry like I told him to. That was a LIE! Truth was she had bruised David's arms and burned him with a cigarette. All dad had to do was look, there was no laundry to be done. Instead he took me to the bathroom, then used his belt to teach me a lesson.

Mom was in school, so when we made it home in the afternoons, we had chores to do. I had to cook, while David did whatever he needed to do. Then we did our homework. It had gotten so bad for David I started doing his homework, signing his papers and even his report cards. She was an ok stylist, but, not near as good as I am. Dad took in the carport, made it into her shop. Sue's Hair Fashions! They had gone to Baton Rouge for mom to take her first test, so I called Dad's sister to come over. We showed her our bruises and told her some of what had happened. She took us to one of her friend's house, so our neighbors would not see the police car drive up. The police men came in. Saw all of our bruises, listened to what we had to say, then asked a few questions. Unless someone sees this happening, they could do nothing. That us being two teen boys we could have done this to ourselves. She drove us home and promised she would talk to dad. The very next week she did. She told him everything we had told her. That she had seen our injuries herself and what the police had said. When dad came home, he sat us all in the living room, then told mom everything our aunt had said. Mom grabbed me by my hair, then started punching me in my face.

David tried to pull her off of me, then she turned on him. We were screaming for dad to help us. He just sat there, looking at the television. It wasn't even on. He did NOTHING! We both missed a week of school to heal. My dear aunt said how very sorry she was for years to come.

I decided to run away, I figured I would have a better chance surviving on the streets. I took the car keys, went out the back door and stole the car. Mom reported the car stolen, a police car pulled in behind me on Interstate 20 west at wells rd. Turned his lights on and his siren. I punched it and finally ran out of gas 100 miles down the road. Bossier City Police, Louisiana State Troopers, Monroe Police and Shreveport Police snatched me out of the car and beat my ass. Took me to juvenile detention, I was still a minor. Mom and Dad came to get me and POOF I was in the court system. Very near this time the state troopers and the Bossier City police killed a white kid who ran from them after he stopped and had given up. Beat him to death. I did not cause any accidents, no one except for me was hurt and I reached speeds in excess of 120 mph. I am not bragging, I wish I had it to do all over again, I can say I never have gotten another ticket to this day.

So I have a lawyer and it is court day. The judge asked me why I ran. I said because no one was ever going to hit me again. He said when I look at you all I see is a spoiled, punk, brat. Turns out because my body was so bruised and battered after they beat me, along with some of mom's handy work my sentence was lessened to seven months unsupervised probation. David was nowhere to be seen at the courthouse either. Mom knew he was bruised worse than me. Dad sat there and once again said nothing. When we got home David was so happy to see me. He asked me to please never leave him again. Sadly I was and I had no idea it was going to happen.

Chapter 5

I was asleep in my room. The door flies open and these two men grab me. Mom and dad are in the hallway. I didn't know what was going on and was asking who they were and what was happening. Dad just said go with them James, they are going to help you. So I did, there was a van in the driveway, I walked up to it in my PJs and bare feet. There was a woman in the back, I sat in the middle, the two men in the front. It wasn't like in the movies where they drive up, snatch someone and drive away. There were no handles inside to where I could open the door. I asked where we were going. One man up front turned around and said shut up faggot! I did. As we backed out of the driveway I had no idea what was about to happen to me. We drove through my neighborhood, to the on ramp of I-20 west. I knew the landmarks from my police chase and the many trips we had taken to Shreveport. After we passed Arcadia the woman in the back put a black hood over my head. I asked her PLEASE tell me, what are you going to do. She said you just don't need to see where we are going. I started to cry and was scared to death. I know we left the interstate because the ride got rough. Finally we stop, she pulls the hood off. It was dark out and cold. There was a cinder block building, a fence, a double door with a light above it. We went into a hallway I would say about 15 feet in there was a door on the left. There were two men standing in front of it. We go in, one says strip. I was terrified but, I did as he said. There was a shower stall, he said shower now with this soap. It stunk, was not like the soap we had at home. So I showered with four men and one woman watching. He handed me a towel, I dried. Another said raise up your arms. I did, then he used a gloved hand to reach into a bag, then he threw this white powder on me. Said turn and did the same to my backside. Another man handed me a jumpsuit. It was tan and had snaps up the front and the back. We walk back into the hallway to a door on the right, there was a covered walkway to another building. I am barefoot and shaking from the cold and fear. One man says once inside you are not allowed to speak to anyone and I mean anyone, you hear me queer? Yes sir I answered. He unlocks the door, we walk into what looked like a warehouse. I am not good with dimensions but it was huge. Inside were cages made of chain-link, like our fence at home. Each had a chain link door very similar to a gate and on each gate there was a lock. There were at least 50 cages and most had someone in it. They lead me to an empty cage, open the door and tell me to go in. I could hear crying and I smelled what I thought was a backed up sewer. Inside the cage there was a cot and some chain that was threaded through the chain link ceiling or top of the cage. On each end of the chain, there were some sort of straps. There was no mattress for the cot, no pillow and no blanket. There were no toilets either. They close the door then click on the lock. I sat on the cot and after I heard them lock the outside door. I asked the boy in the cage next to me. What is this place? Well it didn't take long until the outside door opened and all the lights came on. To my cage they ran. I was so scared. They unlocked and opened my door. A man had a snow white bible. It was hardbound looked to be leather, I will never forget it because I had never seen a bible that white before. Dad had one but it was more of an eggshell tone. Eggshell, oh that just proves how gay I really am!! I backed up to the wall of the cage, as he ran at me with the bible held high. He struck me on top of my head, then once across the right side of my face, then the left. I could taste my blood in my mouth and feel it running down my chin. I stood up and started to try and fight back. He screamed OH NO DEMON YOU WILL NOT RESIST!! I stopped. Did I have a demon in me I thought? They pulled off my jumpsuit, then put the straps hanging from the ceiling around my wrists. Secured them with four zip ties each. They were very tight. I was shaking, bleeding, I was able to stand, but, that was all. I had to have been in shock because I felt no pain at all. The sun came up, went back down and then up again before they released me from the straps. I had used the bathroom on myself, number one and number two, I was exhausted. I was taken back to the shower, I washed myself. Then was given another jumpsuit. I had to get help putting it on because I forgot to snap the snaps in the back. I was taken past the door that lead to the warehouse further down the hall to an office. There was a man I would guess in his late 40's sitting behind an old metal desk. Two men stood beside me, one on either side as I sat in a chair. He said as far as I was concerned he was God and that I had no chance of escape. He wasn't talking to me, he was addressing the demon inside me. That everything was a privilege here right down to a single drop of water. From there I was taken to a room with no windows, there was a claw foot tub in the middle, it was not attached to any plumbing. It was about half full of water and ice. I had to take off my jumpsuit and get in the tub. It was so cold and my feet were already blue from standing so long on the cold concrete in my cage. This man explained the only way to weaken the demon was for me to suffer physical pain. So in order for me to be saved, I was going to suffer. I thought I was used to it, they quickly showed me I wasn't. The ice baths were almost a daily event, along with prayer, as the staff laid hands on me. I was taken to my cage, reminded to not speak and was able to get some sleep. My cot was wet from them spraying the floor from when I had used the bathroom on myself... I was in my third day and had not eaten anything. I had been given water. I had no idea what was coming next. I was taken from my cage to a new room. There was a large wooden table, I call them moving straps, attached to a come along and the straps were about a foot apart. I was told to lay on my back, they strapped me down and then had a pretty big wash cloth or dishtowel crammed in my mouth. I remember it being dry. There were several men in the room, they were praying out loud. One was standing by some sort of machine on a rolling cart. He wheeled it over and was standing at the end of the table at the top of my head. He was wearing thick black gloves, I could see he had something in both hands. As the other men held up their bibles and started speaking in tongues, all of a sudden I felt the shock hit my head. It was awful and I had never experienced anything like this before. It freaking hurt, I could smell burning hair. Yes back then I had hair! I thought I was going to throw up, with that rag in my mouth. A few moments later, BOOM, it happened again. Remember I am strapped down and can't move. He wheels the cart away. I am dizzy and shaking uncontrollably. All leave the room except one. There are no windows and very little light in the room. He is standing on my left side near my head. He removes the cloth from my mouth. He replaces it with an oval ring, it was hard plastic, almost like a small cut of PVC pipe. I could not close my mouth, just bite down on the ring. He climbs on the table with me, puts his knees on either side of my head. Then sits back on my chest. He pulls his penis out of his sweat pants, then says here it comes. He urinated on my face, up my nose and in my mouth. When he was finished he punched me in my stomach to force me to swallow. I passed out. There will be more about this room later.

As I was told everything here was a privilege. To eat or get water I had to earn points. Sometimes it was cleaning or they would make us do something to another kid there. Mostly it was punch or spit on them. Sometimes we had to have sex with one another. One time I was made to poop, on someone's head. I remember there was a boy that was tied to the wooden table. He looked like he was sleeping, but, he was actually unconscious. I had to clean up his vomit and where he had crapped himself. They made me watch as they counted how many ball point pens they could fit in his anus. All of this happened to me while I was there as well.

We are still not allowed to talk to each other, several nights a week they would play loud gospel music, plus, keep the lights on to make it impossible for us to sleep. At least once a week it was a group punishment for us to me sprayed down with a water hose while locked in our cages.

Past the office where I had gotten my first pep talk, there was a hallway to the right. There were two doors, one on either side of the hall. The first one I was taken to was on the left. There was a chair in the center of the room. Not like any chair I had ever seen before. There are metal rings all over it, I am about to find out what they are used for. Where my hands would go there was a cut out in the shape of a hand. The rings were for the straps to secure me. They were about three inches apart and I was strapped in from my neck to my ankles. The strap around my neck made me look up towards the light fixture. I was told to open my fingers, I felt them being secured to the cutout with zip ties. I know it was zip ties because of the sound. ZIP.... ZIP... etc. One man was praying, then inches from my face, he would scream at the demon inside me. Every so often he would hit me in the head with his bible. Then another came over and pushed his hand back on my forehead. He shoved this round piece of wood in my mouth like a horse bit. He did not stop pushing back on my forehead screaming for this demon to leave my body. I felt someone around my right hand, then pain like I have never felt before. They used a rubber mallet to pound round toothpicks underneath my fingernails. Did not stop until the toothpick came through the top part of the nail. Meanwhile they are all screaming for the demon to show itself. They did two to four nails a session, either on my hands or feet. After the toothpicks were pulled out they put a cream on them, covered the nail with a Band-Aid, then I was taken back to my cage. Sometimes dragged because I could not walk. One evening two men come to my cage, open the door, then pull me out by my arm. I smelled whiskey, I know this smell well because of my mom. They take me to the room where I had been shocked. They strap me down, I was terrified. One put the plastic ring back in my mouth. I struggled, but, there was no way I could stop them. They both took off their pants, had erections, then by climbing on the table with me, used my throat and mouth to finish themselves off. This happened so many times. I can't begin to tell you all of the shame and guilt I still carry around with me to this day. I wish I could say it was over, but, it was not. Many times the same two men would bring me to this room, tie me down and rape me. No lubrication, no romance, just forced entry. It felt like I was being ripped apart. I would bleed from my ass for hours. I now understood why all the children here were so quiet and lifeless. It was bone chilling fear. In the other room across the hall, I was to learn a new type of therapy. I would be tied down naked, someone would tape exposed wires to different parts of my body. From my genitals to my head. Then I was shown slides from a projector. Dog, man and woman, two men kissing. BAM they would shock the shit out of me. Kitten, tree, penis and them BAM again. This went on for hours. I still have scars on my inner thighs. Reminders that I was assumed to be damaged and that God would never love me. Not every time I went into the toothpick room did they take off nails. Sometimes they would beat me with their bible's and scream what a piece of shit I was along with other catchy little ditties. I did lose all my finger and toe nails over the 17 weeks. They all grew back over time, but, they don't look like they did before. The final part of the therapy only happened to me one time. I was taken to the table in the shock room, strapped face down with two large pillows placed under my hips to make my butt stick up into the air. My legs were spread before those straps were tightened. I was so afraid of what was coming next. I thought with five men being in the room I was about to be gang raped. I was penetrated but, not by a penis. All the items they did this with gradually got larger until I had a glass coke bottle inside me. I am sure from the conversation these men were making videos of every disgusting thing they did to us.

This is all I can type about what happened to me at the hands of these monsters. My mind simply has to stop.

I was brought my clothes, told to shower, then dress. I was thin when I arrived, but, now I was sick looking. My PJ's just hung off of me. I was taken back to the office with the metal desk. The same man who talked to me the first time was going to again. He said I had a very powerful demon in me and that my parents needed to send me to another place that could deal with it. A tougher camp. He said I was putting the other kids at risk because I did not have enough faith in God to be cured. I was told God and my family hated me. That all they did here was try to help me, to never speak of the treatment. That it was me who let God down. That they would have to bring David here and do the same things to him if I said anything. Was told I was responsible for my entire family's souls that they would burn in hell forever because of me. The lady that rode in the back of the van put a hood back over my head, we drove away. Once back on Interstate 20 East it was removed. At my house they didn't even turn into the driveway. Put me out on the street and drove away. I ran to the door, I guess the parents knew I was coming home. My dad met me at the door. Dad said to me, you are not welcome here, that I was no longer his son. That he had done all he could to save me. That the 25 thousand dollars he spent on me going to conversion therapy was wasted. The therapist, if one could call them that, told dad I didn't even try. That I did not want to get rid of my demon. He handed me a small suitcase that had some clothes in it, then sent me away. The first 2 days I did go to a local church that had a soup kitchen for the homeless. They always had to talk to someone before they would serve them. When I told the pastor why my family put me out, both times he told me that there was nothing there for me and to leave. I was starving. He said he was a man of God, but, didn't act like one. Years later he was thrown out of his church for touching little girls.

Chapter 6

I roamed the streets for the first few days, I slept under an outdoor stairwell at an elementary school. Dad was working in a local welding shop, I walked there one morning to ask for some food. He gave me five dollars to buy something to eat, then said for me to come back around three o'clock. I walked away. I returned at 2:45, sat by the tire of his truck and broke down. I was so hurt, I didn't know what to do. I was just put through pure hell. How I was treated by my parents, by my classmates, my teachers. Not to mention Jesus camp. I was giving up on life. Dad's shift ended at three, he drove me to where I had hidden my suitcase, then to our house. David was so happy to see me. We hugged and he said I love you little bro. I told him I loved him too. He told me mom didn't hit him anymore and she just stayed in her room. Mom was not the same person as when I had been taken away. She was so far gone in her mind, she was having conversations with her dead parents. Like they were sitting next to her on the bed.

I go back in time to when mom was finishing beauty school. She was drinking and popping Valium like crazy. Dad was out of state working, mom was still molesting me. For a short time our cousin, mom's brothers' son, was living with us. My uncle never really did settle down and hitch hiked all over the nation. My cousin had gotten a job, he was nice and we all loved him. Mom went through one of her mental breaks, around the time she was studying for her final state board test. She was throwing all of her beauty tools out the back door, drunk as a skunk. She made a dart down the hall, opened the closet door, this is where dad kept his MANY guns. Took a rifle into her room, then locked the door. To David and me this was a normal day, but, our cousin had never seen her act this way. It was close to the time for dad to come home from work, as usual, we had seen all of this before. She was going to kill herself, again and I still had to finish the potato salad for dinner. Our cousin was banging on her door, begging her not to do it. Just as David and I had 100 times in the past. We were so used to it we just carried on as normal. All the other times when she did come out of her room we were slapped around because we had not finished our chores. So dad drives in, our cousin runs out the door to get him. The difference is she actually shot the rifle. Not at herself mind you, but shot out her bedroom window. Dad went in, took the gun away from her, put it back in the closet. Then back into the bedroom, shut the door. Our cousin was so upset he got in his car to go for a drive. His poor nerves were shot.

I could hear mom and dad fighting, then clear as a bell I hear mom say. DO YOU LOVE HER? Then calling him every name in the book. My all-time favorite was and I quote. "Chief Wrinkle Dick". She comes out of the bedroom and down the hall skipping, Chief wrinkle dick won't fuck his squaw. Out the front door, then around the front yard repeating her little ditty over and over again as loud as she could. I went ahead and mixed her a drink, I knew she would need one as soon as she came back inside. This was the most exercise she had, had for years. I went heavy on the whiskey just like she liked it. She made it back in the house, thanked me for the drink and sat down at the dining room table. I was bringing the food to the table, David was getting the flatware and we were about to have dinner as only the Swift's could. Mom's birthday was approaching soon, I was going to get back in her good graces and cook all her favorites, along with a banana nut cake. That morning she was still in her room, even before I was taken away I had to call all of her clients from her appointment book to tell them she was sick, or some excuse for them not to come. So now the shop was closed forever. I had just taken the cakes out of the oven to cool when she called out for me to please bring her a drink. Her Dr. the week before said no more nerve pills and she was in heavy withdrawals. When he did I thought to myself, this should be interesting! I took her the drink and she said sit with me a minute. I sat on the bed, the door was open so if I had to I could run. She took me by the hand and said I am sorry. Then she said I love you very much. I told her I loved her too. She said send David in. I did and she said the same thing to him.   I had to take David to school, then pick up some groceries. After missing so much of the school year there was no need for me to go back till the next year. Mom didn't drive anymore unless we were going to visit her sister. And my job then was to keep her drinks coming from the back seat. I stopped by to see my aunt, dad's sister, I told her as much about what had happened to me that my shame would allow. It felt good to tell someone. She was amazing, she listened and that was what I needed. We sat and cried together.

Mom always napped from 11am to after 4pm when her stories were on. So when I picked up Dave and went home it was no big deal for her not to be up. I started cooking my special dinner and helped David with his homework. I made stuffed peppers, mac and cheese and a tossed salad. I also iced and decorated the cake. Mom was now 47. She had wanted to be a cake decorator year's back, so we had some nice bags and tips. The one thing I remember about my cake was it leaned. We had asked a couple of her friend to come over, just a couple she still talked with. When the first person arrived, the neighbor from two doors down, mom still hadn't gotten up. I had made a pot of coffee, as I did every day at this time during the week and poured our guest a cup. So I went to gently wake up mom. Remember she is not real fond of being disturbed. When I opened the door I knew something was not right, she was lying in a very awkward position and her arm looked to be a different color. I left the room and closed the door. Dad came home about 10 minutes later. I took him by his arm and lead him to the door of their bedroom. I could not go back in, but he did. He came out of the room, closed the door, looked at me and said. She finally did it. I was numb. His words were empty and I swear I saw joy in his eyes. David was walking down the hall so I stopped him. I said Dave why don't we work on a puzzle, or finish the model car he was building. He loved those and was very good at gluing them together. So he gets the car and I take him into my room. Dad called the police, the one guest went to get her husband. I had other guests showing up, I didn't know what to do so I kept serving coffee. Did not take the police long to get there but to me it seemed like days. Dad was on the couch, David was in my room and I was in the kitchen. The officers went to the back of the house. Then they separated the three of us in separate squad cars. They talked to the one neighbor who was there first and sent everyone else away. It is now around 6pm. We all go to the police department, still not seeing each other and the questions started. Why did you kill your mother? I didn't. Did David kill her? No. Did your father kill her? No. This went on until around midnight, then we were reunited in a room together. Poor David looked like a ghost and dad was just dad. The first thing they did when we arrived was take the small round sticky things, then dab them all over me. My hands, face, my clothes. David and dad said they did to them as well. Turns out it was to see if any of us had fired a gun and we had not. They determined she probably shot herself when we left for the school that morning.

Chapter 7

We are all out in left field and now we have to tell everyone. That was a very tough thing to do. We were about to have a million people come to the house, I didn't feel like doing anything. I remember going to McDonalds to get Dave a hamburger the next day. Dad's Sister and brother in law, not the one I liked, were the first to arrive. Sadly this aunt was killed in a car accident just a few weeks later. They went to the funeral home. I was getting our clothes together, making sure everything was clean and pressed for the funeral. More and more people were showing up. I could not wait for mom's sister and her family to show up, along with the aunt that was so kind to me. Finally everyone arrived, I could go to my room and lay down. I needed to cry, but there were no tears. I was angry but calm. I remember mom's family crying and trying to comfort us as best they could. Dad's family was laughing and talking like nothing had happened. My cousin on mom's side said James you have to eat something. I told her I was not hungry. She said I will make you my gumbo. I loved her gumbo so I said ok. One of dad's brothers took phone duty. We had a black wall mounted rotary phone between the kitchen and dining room, with a high chair next to the counter top. With a spiral cord that would stretch from one end of the house to the other. He was a very large man, I wondered if the chair was going to be able to support his weight. The phone rang as I was getting some tea. He answered, then Yep blew her brains out. Then he let out a little laugh. I hated him from that moment on. She may have not been the best mother in the world, but, she was all we had.

The local paper misprinted the time of the funeral, so I dressed early and went in to represent the family. There were a couple of people there and only one showed up from our church. I need to tell y'all about a week before this happened, mom, was kicked out of the church because she smoked cigarettes. They also told her she could not go to the "Place of Safety" with a gay child. To them this was a place that only the members of this church would be sent. God's chosen people, that when the end of the world came, they were the only ones to be spared. All the other people on earth God would kill.

Dad had mom cremated and there would be only one rose on the alter. From us…her family. Well, dad's best friend brought one too. Straight men can screw anything up. We manage to get through it, go home and the people dwindle away. A few days later David asked me if mom was ever going to come home. I said no, but he would always have me no matter what.

The box comes in with the ashes. Well what we thought were ashes, back then there was an acid option as well. So we had a Ziploc bag full of chunks. Dad drove us to Winnsboro, where mom's parents were buried. He took a post-hole digger and in between her parents graves, dug several feet into the ground, then placed the bag in the hole. Then he filled it in. He said BOY'S this is what I want to happen when I am gone. That changed though. His brother gained power of attorney right before dad died and spent thousands on dad's funeral. Right out of dad's bank account.

A few days later dad calls and said he was going to be late coming home, that I just needed to cook for Dave and me. There was nothing to cook. I did manage some pancakes and eggs. He didn't come home at all that night. The next day was Saturday, he did come home after 3pm. I asked if we could please go to Safeway for some groceries. I had been doing the shopping for years, even when I had to ride my bike. I just didn't have any money. So we all go to the store. When we get home he tells us he will be home Monday after work. I said ok and he just drives off. He didn't come home Monday after work, but, the power and the gas were turned off for non-payment. I never did the bills, which was mom's job. Tuesday night he comes home to a dark house with cold water only. He said it would all be ok, that he was just checking on us and would be home the following afternoon. The power and the gas was turned back on, dad came home after work. I figured with all that had happened he had just forgotten the bills. I could not fault him for that. He brings ice cream and cake. I cut the three of us a slice of cake, then serve the ice cream. He said Boys I have a friend I would like to bring over to meet y'all after work. James you cook something nice, David you help him in the house and cut the grass. I asked what he wanted me to fix. He said steaks on the grill, baked potatoes and that stuff I make with tomatoes and corn. Even then we always had a garden in the back yard. So the next day we do as dad requested. He shows up with this WOMAN!! I have the grill going, everything else was ready, I asked how she wanted her steak, then set off to be a good little gay because I had a roof over my head. As I am outside at the grill all I can think about is my mother and these words. Do you love her? I may have been young, with all I had gone through plus watching Gone with the Wind with my mom once a year since birth. I put two and two together and came up with 69. As we are eating she is Aww honey' this and Aww darlin' that. Then she asked dad. Don't you think I should paint these cabinets a different color? Well that got all over this future drag queen, so I gave her my best MOM stink eye. Oh and she picked up on it instantly. Then out of the blue she says, well you boys do know your mom was crazy right? I think I blew a blood vessel in my right eye. Dad laughed and agreed with her. I managed to get through dinner without losing my manners. She offered to help me with the dishes, I said no thank you. I knew this kitchen well, that she would only slow me down. She was looking around, talking about paint, wallpaper and carpet. I finished loading the dishwasher, rolled it to the sink. Hooked it to the kitchen faucet, plugged it in, then started it. Dad was going to take her home, said he would be back later. She gave David a hug, I knew I was next. As she leaned in she said, you do know this is about to be my house don't you? I was furious. I waited up for DARLIN to get in. I know I must have reminded him of mother because I look just like her. I told him what she had said, he agreed. Yes it probably will be hers soon. It is not two weeks since mom died. So I ask how and where you two met. OMG she is his best friends' sister. The best friend of 20 years. The best friend who brought the other rose to mom's funeral!! I believe mom went stupid because dad went stepping out. That David and I were her only outlet for her anger! I understand her so much better now. The new woman would call, if I answered I would just hang up the phone. She had us over for dinner at her parents' house, which by the way she still lived in. She announced before we sat down, that she did not set a fancy table and that they were just regular people. Well fuck you too lady. I used the good dishes to be nice to you! I even threw her plate, glass and flatware in the trash!! How you like me now? The very next week my father sits me down and says. She said either you go or she does and I love her. I said, so once again I am being thrown out? I said I thought we were a family again, then walked out the front door.

I was trying to figure out what I was going to do. It did cross my mind to jump off a roof, or break a window and cut my wrists. Something inside me just said no!! I was walking and somehow ended up in a public park on the Ouachita River. I sat down, was looking at the water. Honestly I did not know what my next move was going to be. I took off my shoes and socks, my shirt and pants, I did keep my navy blue briefs on. Waded out a few feet and splashed the water on me to rinse off my sweat. The water felt nice, but it did smell a little, as river water does. As I was walking back to my clothes I noticed a work van had stopped in the grass very near where I was going to sit. Had a logo on the side along with a phone number. I see the man getting out, as I sat down with my stuff. I was drying off a little with my shirt, he stood near me and asked. How's the water? I answered a little smelly but nice. He had some facial hair, like he had just started to grow a beard. He was white and I would guess in his mid-thirties. He had the build of a working man, broad shoulders and toned muscles. Instantly I thought to pick up my things and run. So I quickly started to dress. He must have picked up on my nervousness because he asked. You in a hurry? I answered not really, I just don't want any trouble. He replied, I am not trouble that he wished I would stay and talk. I think to set me more at ease, he sat about five feet away from me. He started to talk, I learned he was married, that they had two kids, a son 4 years old and a daughter 2. That he was in the park for his lunch break, that he had some sandwiches his wife had fixed, along with some chips. He asked if I was hungry, because he was, that he had plenty to share. I said I am hungry, but I had no money to pay for the food. He said no problem, he stood up and went to his van. He came back with a small cooler and a paper lunch bag. He reached in, pulled out a peanut butter and jelly sandwich along with a small bag of chips, he handed them to me. Before I could ask, he pulled the same out for himself. I wasn't going to accept it if he would not have had anything to eat. In the cooler he had some beer, asked if I wanted one? I said sure, trying to look older than I was. As we ate he asked me if I was in the park alone. And did I live near the park? I said I was alone and I lived a few miles away. Through the chit chat I noticed he kept touching himself in his groin area. That really wasn't strange,

I had seen guys do that all of my life. Like they had to keep checking if it was still there. As if it could had fallen off or something. He asked me if I was in the park looking for something. That some men came to this and other parks looking for something they could not get at home. At first I had no idea what he was talking about. It just went over my head. I had gotten up to throw my trash in the trash can, I asked if he wanted me to take his? He said yes. The trash can was about ten feet away, so off I went. As I approached him from behind and to his right, I noticed he had pulled his penis out and was stroking it right there in the open. I asked are you CRAZY? He said do you like it? I didn't know what to say. I just stood there. He said I want you to touch it, we can get into my van, that way no one will see. I was just about to run like hell, then he said. I will pay you. My heart was pounding, I was scared, but, money I did need. He said I have never seen you out here, which meant he has done this before. He said I am so horny and he liked the way I looked. I asked how much? He said 20 dollars if I would jack him off, forty if I was willing to do more. Well y'all 20 bucks back then would have fed me for many days, so I said ok. He tucked his junk away, stood up, picked up the cooler, we were headed for the van. When he slid the van door shut he reached over and started to rub my crotch. At my age it took 2 seconds for something to happen, He said get them pants off boy! He started giving me oral, plus taking off his clothes. As the mood became more intense he said. I want you to breed me boy! In my head I didn't know what to say, or do. So he gets me to lay on my back, takes control himself by sitting on my erect penis. I just went with it and soon enough it was over. He threw me a rag, we cleaned up. He said to never tell anyone, that he would be looking for me again. He threw me 40 dollars, then said he had to get back to work. I walked straight to the river. Didn't take off anything. I jumped in, I felt so sick to my stomach, threw up the lunch I had just eaten. I thought James you are going to bust hell wide open now. I laid on the grass to let the sun warm and dry me. I had 40 dollars so I knew I would eat. That I could get more clothes at garage sales. I remembered he said other men were looking for the same. So I guess I had a job now. I hadn't even started shaving yet, so I figured they liked young guys. As the sun began to set, I noticed many cars just driving through the park. It was odd that each car or truck only had one man in them. They just drove through the park over and over again. There were picnic tables set up, so I picked out one near the road and sat down facing it. Sure enough a Lincoln pulled over. This man rolled down the window, then motioned for me to come over. He asked if I was having a nice evening. I said sure. He asked what are you doing out here? I said just enjoying the park. He asked you want to go for a ride? I said sounds good to me. I stepped into the car on the passenger side then off we went. The Lincoln was new, I loved the smell. I told him I like your car. He said thanks. We had driven a few miles into West Monroe, so I asked if he was going to take me back to the park. That I was meeting friends later. He said yes and for me not to worry. He was an older man, at least 50, had thinning gray hair. It was a comb over, I had seen a few in mom's shop. I was laughing a little inside. We stop at a small house in a not so nice looking neighborhood. The smell of the paper mill was very strong, so I knew we had to be close to it. Smelled like rotten eggs. There was an older Ford pickup truck parked beside the house, he said I have a friend I want you to meet. So we left the pretty Lincoln then walked through the side door of the home. There was an unmade bed in the center of the room, a ripped up chair with a towel over the seat. One lamp that was on a small table by the bed and a box fan blowing the warm air around. The other man walked out of the kitchen area, he wasn't wearing a shirt. He had gray chest hair, I would say he was in his mid-forties. He said well let's take a look get naked. So as I undressed they did the same. The man from the Lincoln said GET HIM. The other man grabbed me, then threw me on the bed. I was face down. He sat his ass on my head and was holding my arms with his knees. Then Mr. Comb over spit on my ass and plowed in. I screamed in pain, they laughed. As he raped me the other man started to punch me in my kidney area and it hurt like hell. Comb over said hit him again, it gets real tight when you do. So he kept hitting me. They switched I did not resist, I just wanted it to be over and not to be killed. When they were done, the man with the gray chest hair, turned me over then punched me in my jaw. I was knocked out. I woke up in some bushes, near very tall trees. I was dressed and in pain. I took off my shoe to see if I still had my 40 dollars. Huge relief, it was still there. Was so dark out, not a soul to be seen. I stood up, walked around and then realized I was in the park on the west side of the river. I was bleeding as I did in the therapy compound. I remembered when my aunt had called the police, they said if no one saw it, it was like it didn't happen. So I went back into the river to clean myself up and rinse out my clothes. I dressed, went to a bench, tried to sleep. The next morning when I had to pee it scared me because there was red blood mixed in. I stayed the day and night, until I could walk better and needed something to eat. The cycle of being with men from the parks went on for many months. Most were ok, but I did have a few that I wondered if I would survive. I was thinking I had to get off the streets, I had to be able to support myself without this BULLSHIT! I decided to walk to the beauty school my mom went to. I needed to know what it would take for me to start. The financial aid lady was so nice. She told me of a program that would pay me to go to school if I kept my grades up. There were requirements I needed to meet first though. I had a new plan, I didn't have to be a whore forever.

Chapter 8

Dad sees me walking on Louisville Ave, he turns into a parking lot. He is in the new Cadillac he had bought for my stepmother. Y'all need to know mom died on May 17th. Dad remarried July 4th. So all of this happened in a very short time. He asked me how I was. I cursed him with the last of my stank breath I could muster. I told him I needed to go to beauty school or get some kind of training. That I was too young to have a tax return and that the financial aid people said I needed an address for the J.T.P.A. program and grants. He said Let me ask her and I will see! On HELL no! I walked away. The first pay phone I came to I called his sister. I told her how I was living, then what my dad had said. She asked where I was, I told her. She said she could meet me the next day. We set a time and a place. When she picked me up, we drove straight to my father's house. She didn't even knock on the door just opened it and walked in. The front of the house was empty. She said BROTHER!! He called out HEY, from the master bedroom. She flew down the hall, opened the door. There they were, laying on the bed watching TV. My aunt called my dad by his first name. She said I want your last year's tax return, I am not leaving this room without it. My stepmother took a breath to speak. My aunt shut her down quick. My aunt told her Please say one word. I have dreamed of kicking your ass ever since you took up with my brother. Dad looked upset, his sister said. You have something to say? He just handed her the tax papers. She said, I didn't think so. Spun around slammed the bedroom door and really slammed the front door as we walked out of the house. I move in with my aunt. She gets me to and from school. I am thrilled to have some of the same instructors mom had. Also I beat her on every test score she took. I gave my aunt all of the grant money that was left over from my tuition and my checks weekly from the J.T.P.A. To cover me living there. I kept my tips. Sadly though, when I desperately needed money, I would return to the parks. I took a knife with me on those dates and yes a couple times I had to use it. I saw light at the end of the tunnel and GOD himself could not stop me.

I work in a couple salons in the mall, but, getting to and from Winnsboro was tough without a car. 30 miles one way was just too far to walk. Then my aunt loses the house she was renting. I had not been out of school long enough to build a clientele, so I decided while I was still young and cute. I needed to move to the only city in the state I could be gay. New Orleans.

So I take the bus to New Orleans. No place to stay, didn't know a soul. In the French Quarter it was very easy for me to sell myself. There were even bars that boys for hire liked to hang out in. Being a new face didn't hurt. I learned a new term as well. Gay for pay. There were straight guys as well. They would have gay sex, only if they were paid the right amount of money. I guess everyone has their price. I hustled up enough money in one night to pay the weekly rate at a cheap motel some of the boys told me about. I was lucky on those streets. I wasn't murdered, because some were, the very night I was out there doing the exact same thing. I was going to start my life. I call the house from time to time and if anyone except David answered I would just hang up. Finally he answered and it just so happened he was home alone. We have a great talk. He was telling me how he was tending to our stepmothers mother who had moved in. And that one of her sons had moved into my old room. He was in his 30's!! So dad kept my brother to be slave labor. David said my aunt wanted me to call as soon as I could. That a friend of mine stopped by the house to see me, since I wasn't there Dave gave him our aunt's phone number. That dad and Bitchzilla did not know my friend had come by.

So I call her next, tell her where I was living. Catch up on family gossip. She told me David was going to special classes at the local university N.L.U. Now it is U.L.M they were going to help him. Then she said I have a message for you from a very nice guy maned C.K. I almost fainted. She gave me his telephone number, then we said our goodbye's. I could not dial fast enough! I was so very happy to hear his voice again. He told me that he missed me. That he thought about me every day. We are reconnected, I was over the moon.

Talking to the desk clerk at the cheap motel I was staying in, I learned everyone who worked there had to live on the property. That got me to thinking. So I land a job at the motel, just so happened they did need someone in housekeeping and the front desk. David had started the program for learning disabled kids. He was paired with a speech therapist and others to help him develop more. His speech lady was a Yankee and some of his word's he still says with a northern accent! I just love that! He excelled in this environment, I was so very proud of him. Was about 8 months in when the Autism Spectrum terms came into my life.

I was living in New Orleans, enrolling in makeup and massage school. Had the motel as my home, I was thrilled to have a roof over my head, phone, running water, air conditioning and heat! Was humble, but, I was living. I had a plan, get all my licenses, do some bootleg hair at the hotel, then go to work in a glamorous salon. My friends were bartenders, drag queens, hookers and drug dealers. There is a complete second book I could write about them. And how one amazing Lady saved me from drugs. But that is later.

I had no problem with any of them, they were real people, kind to me and my new support group. Not only did I have a place to live, I also made 20 dollars a shift on the desk and another 20 for a shift housekeeping. I was rich!! The days were crazy. I went to school in the morning, cleaned rooms in the afternoons and the night audit grave yard shift behind the desk. I was young so this was no problem. It would kill me now. I talked to David almost daily and once a week to C.K. He was going to join the Marines. I knew one day we would be together. We were dating, never have had sex and had only kissed a few times. I guess this should have shown me I was never going to have a normal life. Things are looking up and I am crazy enough to think I can change the world.

Months later I call my aunt, needed to catch up on family drama, also to see how she is doing. She was having bad headaches, the doctors found cluster tumors in her head. She said she was on medications and was very happy I called. Dad was going to put David in a home. I guess he needed to erase as much of his old life as possible, so he could fit her and her 5 grown sons in his new one. I believe dad was her 5th marriage. I thought about the place he had sent me, No this just wouldn't do.

The owner of the motel was an interesting man. He was married, wealthy and loved sex with young athletic jock boys. There was no shortage of them in New Orleans. With runaways, young people who were down on their luck, or just trying to make ends meet. I was tall, thin and somewhat handsome. But butch, I have never been. That worked in my favor because he wasn't attracted to me. I was efficient in my work, from the laundry, housekeeping and the front desk. He said I added a touch of class to the place. Made me feel good. There were four of us who worked the front desk. We were 13 blocks from the French Quarter, charged $24.99 a night and we had a weekly rate as well. The other housekeepers and bellman were a constant flow of kids trying to make it in a tough world. I was always training someone to do something around the place. The building at one time had been very grand. Inside courtyards with a huge pool. All inside a 30 foot block wall. We had off street parking with only one way in and out, through the lobby. If someone staying with us brought back a guest for the evening, there was an eight dollar charge for them to get on the elevator. Either they paid it, or they left. This made for some very interesting evenings behind the desk for sure. There were no rooms on the ground floor. The parking garage, lobby, pool, along with a closed restaurant. The rooms were second and third floor. They were in constant need of some kind of repair. There was a water cooled AC system and the pipes were a nightmare. There were two maintenance workers when I started, but, one was fired. That really meant he was just thrown out on the street. The owner never did this, it was always a call to the front desk, or to one of our rooms with instructions to get rid of so and so. Either they stole something, did too many drugs, drank too much or didn't work hard enough. Sometimes when the owner was done with his conquest of getting what he wanted from a guy he had us to throw them out. He had to have been bipolar as well as bisexual. Sometimes his behavior reminded me of my mom. He would come in at 2 am, with some guy he picked up in a bar or on the street. Would walk up to the desk and ask for his key. Those guys never knew he owned the place. We were to treat him as a guest. Sometimes he would get me to go into the known hustler bars, where men could be bought for sex, to pick someone out for him. Well I guess pick up. He was older and had gotten a reputation around the Quarter for being an ass and a jerk. In the years I worked and lived there I never saw nor spoke to his wife. I would tell the guys my uncle was in town, that he was too embarrassed to come in the bar. That he had never been with a man and that he was interested in paying for the experience. It never failed

Believe it or not we were actually pretty busy. We had 100 rooms, even in their older state they were clean. Thanks to me and affordable. Not one time while I worked there were we robbed or was I really scared while working.

Chapter 9

We were down a maintenance worker, I wanted David with me. I could not stand the fact after him telling me he had changed my stepmother's mother adult diapers. That my spineless father was going to put him in a home. So I started saving money for David a bus ticket. I talked to the owner, he said he would hire him for a 3 week trial and if all went ok he could stay. I called the house, it just so happened dad answered the phone. I told him I was working, in school, had a place to live and wanted David to move in with me. He said well I am not driving him anywhere. I had figured as much. So I asked if he could manage to drive him to the bus station. I would have a ticket waiting for him. He said GLADLY! I asked to speak to my brother. He called Dave to the phone. I asked would you want to come live with me. He didn't even ask where, just a big YES!! I was thrilled. I told him he would have to work in the motel with me, but he would have his own room adjoining mine, his own bathroom and television. That he would also make 20 dollars a day. I told him whatever he brought with him we had to carry many blocks from the station, so pack as light as he could. I couldn't even afford a cab! So I set out as soon as he hung up the phone to buy his ticket. The next day he arrived. The night before I pulled the best furniture I could find out of the storage rooms, cleaned everything, made the bed, set my big bro up with a bachelor pad! I made it to the station just as he arrived. There he was and he didn't care who saw, he gave me a big hug with tears in his eyes. We managed to carry all of his things back to the motel. He met the owner that night and started working the next day. His coworker was a nice guy, in his 30's. Turned out he was hiding from the law up north, but, that was nothing new for us. We were an unconventional group who looked out for each other.

David picked up on everything he needed to and was a great worker. I was studying with him to get his G.E.D. If I had have used my brain I should have gotten mine at the same time. I was already in two classes and working double shifts. When the time came for him to test, my dear aunt drove down, picked him up, he tested where he could get the diploma from the parish school we had attended. He passed and oh how very proud I was of him. Still am every day.

As I was saying the motel owner was off his rocker. Sometimes he would come in on my night shift in a panic. Get everyone up James. We have too many rooms offline, they have to be fixed tonight. We would have 45 vacant rooms, but, that didn't matter. So I would call everyone on the switchboard. Those of us who worked behind the desk didn't have to help. He needed the ones he trusted to like him because we handled the money. I am sure in that kind of setup he had been stolen from many times. David had an adjustment to this because it was not structured and a few times he almost got us thrown out. He would listen to me, so we got past that. Soon enough he was quite like everyone else, just trying to stay and survive.

This is one thing that happened while we were there. I was working my shift behind the desk, I had finished the night audit and then I was to lock the cash drawer, go out of the lobby and walk through the parking garage just to make sure all of the cars were registered to our guests. As I was finishing I walked to the entrance on Tulane Ave. Just before I was to the sidewalk I heard glass breaking and one of our chairs fell out in the street. There was no traffic, thank goodness so I grabbed the chair, looked up to see which room it had come from. I went back in, called David and his coworker to tell them what had happened. Many times we had to remove a guest for being too loud, drunk, hustling the other guests or other sordid reasons. This was just a day in the life. Now the broken window was a little out of the ordinary. The guys came down to get the master key and investigate. They go up and in the room. The guest was just going crazy tearing up the room. They wrestle him to the floor, a gun falls out of his belt. This was very scary for me to hear. They hold him down, I had already called the police. They were right down the street so it didn't take long for them to arrive. They arrest the man, take his gun, his baggage and a copy of his bill. We had to record some sort of driver's license or ID for someone to rent a room. He had told the police he didn't have one. David comes down with a duffle bag he had found under the bed. The guest said it wasn't his, so I figured one of our top notch housekeepers forgot to look under the bed. I told the police I would put it in lost and found to see if anyone would claim it. What that really meant was if something fit David or me we scored a new outfit. I unzipped the bag, it was full of MONEY! At that second as hard as our lives were, I could have kept my mouth shut and we could have slipped away in the night. That wasn't me though. I always try to do the right thing. I asked an officer to come over, opened the bag and showed him what was in it. The man had robbed a bank up North, then fled to New Orleans. There was a story in the paper, most called me crazy for giving the money over. I would like to say the bank sent a reward, a card, or called but they did nothing. The police did let me know the money was unmarked and would have been untraceable. UGG! I knew where I was, I knew some of the dealers in the neighborhood and let's just say we had some organized people as well. I wasn't going to steal from someone who could make us disappear without a trace. I played it smart and safe. It wasn't just me, I had David to look out for too. It was the only time in my life I held over 20 thousand dollars in my hands. Ok back to me now!! I was in makeup school our homework assignments were now application technique. We were given a Polaroid camera, some film it would spit out and a flash bar. We were to do someone's makeup in whatever the homework style was. Take a photo then turn it in the next day. I really didn't have anyone being as the classes were in the morning, my circle of friends worked nights and lived in the hotel as either an employee or long term guest. So I would paint my face, take the picture, turn it in the next day. One day I was finished with my housekeeping and I had some time until I had to work the night shift at the desk. So I painted my face, by chance one of the drag queens stopped by to borrow a cassette tape. We were so high tech. She saw my makeup then said on no honey you are not going to wash that paint job off. She called down a couple other show girls and they got busy fast. I am 6 feet tall, learned I wore a women's size 7 dress, size 11 shoe and needed clip on earrings. I called the owner of the motel, said I was not feeling well. He said find someone to cover your shift. One of the queens' boyfriend also worked the desk. He said he would if I gave him the 20 dollars when we got paid. I agreed, that was that. They took some spandex, it was hot pink, cut it, put a seam up the back, BOOM and I had a dress. Put a wig on me, the lowest pair of heels that would fit. We shaved off the 4 chest hairs I had at the time, then came the stockings, nails, bra stuffed with dry beans in a pair of knee highs and some jewelry. First the earrings and my dear friend took out her best necklace. It had been grand, had some age, but she was offering me the best she had. She said it may be a rusted rhinestone necklace, but in the light she still shines like a diamond. I have always thought of that statement. How I had been treated by those who were supposed to protect me. It just fit. Even though someone may be older, little rough around the edges or different. There is no need to write them off, or throw them away. Because in the right light we can all shine like a new diamond. My online family taught me that as well. Big hug's y'all!!

Ok, I was looking like Barbra, so I was going to sing Sweet Inspiration. Karaoke was not invented yet, so I would have to sing along with the tape. I stumbled the 13 blocks to the Quarter in those heels and then to the little bar on North Rampart St. I was nervous but excited. The other queens looked at me. Some were title holders and saw no competition at all. One did a gesture like she was picking her nose. That meant booger. A booger queen was usually not pretty and looked a hot mess. Worse than booger you were called a brick. Being a brick just meant you were only pretty in pitch darkness. I met the owner of the club, he as well was a queen, but much older. His partner of 30 years right by his side. I introduced myself as James. She said, that is not a good drag name and you pretty much got it from the neck down. That stung y'all. I just wanted to go home. My hooker drag friends would not let me. I was last on the list to perform and the prize was 50 dollars. I really wanted to win, it was not rare for David and me to have less than 10 dollars between us at all times. We had shelter, food and were young enough to feel like we had it all and were on top of the world. Even to this day, David will see me at my desk working on our bills and say. We are making it. Like we used to say back then, it does warm my heart. Ok the other queens do their numbers, lip sync, their costumes were amazing. I was so nervous when they called me to the stage. Everyone else had a drag name so they called me Ms. Understood. There I was in a make shift dress, rusted jewelry, a used wig and borrowed shoes. Some in the crowd laughed, my friends from the motel were just screaming and clapping. They also had heard me sing before. The music starts, I start singing and I was in the zone. Everyone in the bar stood up and went crazy. There were In Living Color snaps, high fives, a feeling I will never forget settled over me. I walk out into the crowd, keep my song going and I really feel the blisters on my feet now! The song ends with a bang. People were handing me dollar bills, giving me hugs and screaming You Go Fish! Which meant you go gurl. The roar was overwhelming, the bartenders were throwing napkins in the air and showering everyone by shaking up club soda like it was champagne! I just cried y'all. Ruined my makeup and fell to my knees. My friends take me backstage to do a quick repair job. All of the contestants were brought back on stage, the host was going to hold her hand over each one. Who the crowd cheered the most for would win. When she raised her hand over me, they went crazy again. Sounded like being in the Super Dome after the Saints made a touchdown. I could not believe it, I WON! With the prize money, plus tips I earned 120 dollars that night. I thought this was way better than hooking!! That was a life changing moment and to this day I still get choked up. Mother Bob, the club owner asked me to join the house cast. I am very proud to be her drag daughter.

C.K. had joined the Marines, we were writing back and forth. He had to be careful because being a gay man he was not supposed to be there. In his defense he was not a nelly, messy drag queen like me. I was not much into sex, after the way I was treated by my mom, going to camp and selling myself to survive. I always said after being paid for sex, doing it for free just didn't seem right. C.K. was going to change my thought process on that y'all. I had my hands full with David, the motel and life in a true big city. As the drag shows were becoming more popular we formed a very good little troupe. I finished my training and now was a fully licensed member of the beauty and relaxation culture. I was making money in the clubs, so I gave up my night job at the motel, but still worked housekeeping. I also trained my replacement to do everything as I did. We had a working system that I didn't want to break. With my new popularity the motel owner would come to a few shows, I would help him snag a tourist. Sometimes promote his newest venture, He had turned the suites into youth hostels. I had never heard that word before. He started to advertise. Business was good and we had a solid team at the motel. David was now head of maintenance, with two guys working with him. We had more rooms than ever to rent. In the back of my mind I knew the time to get an apartment was coming. I was making good money in the shows, also was ready to put my training to work in a salon. I was not aware the motel owner was thinking about this too.

So our drag troupe is starting to get coverage in the local press, word of mouth is paying off as well. I take the name Fifi from a fabulous glamour shop in the Quarter that sponsored me with some makeup, wigs and jewelry. Drag is expensive y'all. My sisters are teaching me how to sew, bead, plus my wig skills are really strong.

I have another story to share from the motel. Everyone knew I was doing shows along with two others that lived there. One of the straight guys that worked with us about a year, I will call him Ed. Well he wanted to see a show. But, he had never been to a gay bar and was scared to go on his own. We agree he needed to go on a Thursday night. Was a smaller crowd. So we all pile in a cab three queens and a breeder! Ed asked, will you protect me? We laugh, yes Ed! We sit him at a table next to the stage, load him up with free drink tickets and then go backstage to finish getting ready. I have to say it was an amazing show. We did some Broadway hit songs, then the second act we were a drag queen barber shop quartet. Everything went great plus the tips were good as well. I make my way up front to see how Ed is holding up. He was floored by how good we were and that we sang live. A lady at the bar sent me a drink, so I asked her to join us at the table. She was going on about how pretty I was. She was right to notice. Hehe! She wanted to ask me some questions. I know the 3 she will ask. We get them over and over. #1) when did you know you were gay? When my boyfriend kissed me for the first time. #2) Why do drag? It is fun, pays the bills and as Fifi I can be as outgoing as I want to be and that James was definitely shyer. #3) Have you ever been with a woman? No and I don't count my molestation as being with one. So she asked. How do you know you are really gay? Before I could answer, she said my hotel is two blocks away. Why don't we go and talk for a while? I answered I am in a long term relationship, we only have sex together. We hug and off she goes. Ed asked. Aren't these women gay? I said heavens no. Most women who come see us perform are straight. They like the gay bars to get away from men like you! I could almost see the hamster running the wheel in his brain. We say night night to everyone, jump in a cab and go back to the motel. The next night during one of my numbers, I see Ed walk in. So when we are finished I walk over to him sitting at the bar. How did we look and sound? He said even better than the night before. Just what I wanted to hear, as show director I wanted the best damn drag show in town. As the tourist were taking photos with us, sending us drinks and shots, he asked to talk when I had time. I said after the meet and greet we could go backstage. We can't drink all of this alcohol, so we would B drink. The bartenders would charge the customer for what they ordered, fix us water or coke, then at the end of the evening we split the cash with them. Let me tell y'all, it kept Fifi in pantyhose! I needed to freshen up my makeup so I tell Ed to meet me backstage. He did. Then he said I want to meet the blonde at the end of the bar. Will you go over there with me? I said sure. Then he asks, may I hold your hand? Oh that little shit! I knew what he was up to then. First I said, let's go talk to her, then we would figure out our next move. I had picked up guys for my boss, why not a woman for Ed? We walk over, I strike up a conversation. She was from England and loved our production. We talk about Dame Edna, I notice she is looking Ed up and down, so I reach down to take his hand. She asked if we were a couple. I said more like friends. Ed asked me, Fifi have you ever been with a woman? The lady asked us both the same question. I answered that I was 100% gay and no I have not been. Then I said I doubt Ed has been with a woman either. She said really? He was smiling thinking his little scam was working. I said yes and it is really tragic. Ed has the smallest penis I have ever seen in my life. I hadn't seen his penis, doing this act for the owner was out of necessity. I had to have a place to live. I was not going to lie to this woman, even if she was a stranger. I wish you could have seen his face. She and I had a huge laugh, then I bought her a drink. Ed stayed a couple more minutes, then left. I never saw him in the club again. Jackass!

Chapter 10

I am checking out the hair salons in the French Quarter, there is one I just loved. I will call it the shop. All the walls were completely covered in mirrors, beautiful crystal chandeliers, 100% glamor!! I was a perfect fit. The owner hired me on the spot. I had been saving money for about 7 months, so it was time to look for an apartment as well. The first place I went, was a property management office. I sat to talk with the lady. She asked about my income. I told her I had finally finished school. That I did the shows, that I was just hired in a shop as well. I filled out the application, handed it to her and thanked her for her time. I had just gotten out the door, noticed I had left my MURSE in her office. That is a man purse!! Went back in to see her tearing up my paperwork and "prissying" around imitating me. She said with her back to me and I quote. We will never have queers renting from us. She looked at me, I picked up my bag shot her the finger and walked out.

So I decided to keep looking. The very next place I went things were much better. This family owned several apartment complexes in the Quarter. They had a one bedroom, one bath available, it was just two blocks from the shop. It was split level, living room and kitchen downstairs, a spiral staircase, bedroom and full bath upstairs. It was in our budget, plus they welcomed gays to rent. So I signed the lease then she handed me the keys. In one day I had a new job and we had our first apartment. I could not wait to tell David. We needed to pack, this was Saturday and my first day at work was Tuesday. Plus I had my drag shows all weekend. David was so excited to hear my news. I called the owner, left him a message on his answering machine. Later that night the owner called me to his office. He had heard my message. He told me there was money missing, that all fingers pointed to me because of the apartment. I knew he was lying, everyone knew for months I had been saving money for this. He said we couldn't leave until we paid the money back. I told him we didn't have his money and if any was missing I would have heard about it before him. David and I were the 2 that had now been there the longest. To make a long story short I called his bluff.

I called the police, he had no proof there was any money missing, plus the cash drawer was right and the deposits all added up. So the police helped us load what few things we had in a squad car, then drove us to our new home. I thought to myself, another person in my life who just wanted to hurt me. We needed everything to set up house. We had no dishes, furniture, not even a towel. I would put a futon downstairs, which was all the rage back then. And a full-size bed upstairs for me. We had the French Market, tons of second hand stores near us, with all kinds of cheap but awesome finds.

Working in the salon I was making more money than I ever had. I was very proud of myself and of my brother. We had an unbreakable bond. Dave was hired by our new landlords to work in the courtyards of all their complexes. We were finally completely on our own. We had the place furnished and decorated as only an Autistic man and his Drag Queen brother could. Fifi started in pageants, won many and picked up some extra exposure doing local TV commercials in drag. We had the phone turned on and my first call was to C.K. We scheduled a visit, I would have him for a week. I was excited, yet nervous and wanted everything perfect. Also David had met someone as well. She was a bartender in a local gay bar. Straight and so very sweet. It wasn't a show bar, nor did they even want queens in the place. Was more of S and M vibe. There was a sign on the door that said, Wearing Cologne, Do Not Enter. That was me, I applied half a bottle before I stepped out my door! You could smell Ms. Fifi five minutes before she arrived! Dave was cool with C.K. visiting.

We opened a bank account, there was no need yet for a car, the cost of parking alone was more that taking cabs everywhere.

Now one of the queens in the troupe with me, also bartended at Mother Bob's bar. Her name was D.D. She had become my best friend. We went everywhere together. With pageant season approaching we were busy making outfits, teasing wigs, picking and perfecting a talent. We had heard of a store going out of business in Kenner. They sold gowns, they were 80% off. We hail a cab, have cash in our murses and not to mention it takes months to bead a gown by hand. What a time saver. We arrive at the strip mall. I knew I wanted something in blue, or green. I already had shoes for those colors. D.D. wanted black. We go in the store and let the shopping begin. We stayed together so if we found something one of us could hold it up to the others back to see if the shoulders fit. I would say we were in there 15 minutes when the police come in. Walk right up to us. One officer said the owner had called them and that if we didn't leave he was going to charge us with disturbing the peace. The woman walked up, said your kind are not welcome here. I said to the officer that we would leave. Turned to the lady, told her if you would have welcomed our kind, you, wouldn't be going out of business!

The day of C.K.'s arrival was here. The Airport Shuttle would bring people into the quarter much cheaper than a cab, all you had to do was give them the name of the hotel to drop off at. There was one right down the street on ST ANN. He had the name and I was really getting nervous. There were no cell phones, or internet then. We had pay phones and snail mail. I knew what time his flight would be in, I added 45 minutes for the shuttle. So I was standing outside of the hotel about an hour before his flight landed. I know VERY Alice Faye, I just couldn't help myself. I had cleaned our apartment, David had instructions to not mess anything up.

Several shuttles came and went. Seemed like he would never get there. To my joy, right on time, there he was. Lean, muscular and all mine. Well I hoped. It was ok to hug right there on the street, even kiss. We lived in one of the few bubbles where we outnumbered the straight people, even for someone to be elected they had to swing our vote. All we did was a quick hug. Could it be that I was going to have the Cinderfella story? It sure did seem that way.

We walked the short distance to the gate to our apartment, I keyed in our code. He asked what the buttons were for.   I told him we had an intercom to talk to people at the gate and can even buzz them in. He said Ooooo fancy. I laughed. We were past the stairwell and just 2 doors down. We had hurricane shutters we could close over the french doors, up and down stairs. They were also on the two windows. Dave had been called to work, so we went upstairs to catch up. We talked about everything we couldn't over the phone. I had already decided I would tell him everything that had happened to me and what I had done to survive. I hoped he would understand, not just throw me away like trash. As my words and tears began to flow, he sat still and listened. From time to time he would reach over to hold my hand. When I was finished I asked him to please not judge me and I would understand if he wanted to leave. He took my hand, stood up and had me stand too. His amazing green eyes filled with tears, he pulled me to him, as I stood there. His arms around me, he cried. Not a few tears, many. It was like he felt my pain inside. I knew I was in love with this man. It felt like the weight of the world had been lifted off of me. I was looking down. He placed his finger under my chin to raise it up. He spoke. Your words only draw me closer to you James. That I would never judge you, nor will I ever throw you away. That he did understand. He kissed me. He said well you are still a virgin. I looked at him like he was crazy. He said, because you have never made love. It was nice to have him there. I had to start getting ready for a show. I sent him downstairs so I could shower, shave my pits and legs. The bathroom was small and I needed every available square inch of space. Honestly I was giving him an easy way out if he wanted to leave. I call down to him after I tied on my dressing gown, was thrilled to hear him coming up the stairs. As I do my makeup, he tells me how brutal the other Marines were to the queers they had suspected or found out about. That it would be best if I let him call from now on, so he could always do it from a safe place. He then goes to take a shower. I was so angry at Senators McCain, Helms and Thurmond. Spewing their lies along with every church in America. Civilization as we knew it would stop to exist if gays could serve in the military, or be a teacher, marry, but the truth was, these people had twisted the constitution and laws to fit their beliefs. Liberty and justice for all does not say exclude someone. They don't like losing the power they wrongfully acquired in the first place. Ok rant over, back to me! When he came out of the shower, he had no problem being naked in the room with me. I had never seen him naked. Gurl his muscles were beautiful and so was something else. I almost ruined my tuck! He gets dressed then asked what he could do to help me.

He helps me with my jewelry, then my nails. I pick up my clutch and am ready to go. He says baby, you look like a million bucks! And for the first time in my life I believed it. Before we walked out the door, he gave me a very gentle kiss on my hand. Smart man, DO NOT touch the face once it is painted! Fifi had never had boyfriend come to a show. We walked to the club, about 6 blocks. Along the way we are stopped several times by tourists wanting to take a photo with me. My drag mother always said, be a lady and they will love you. She was right, they did. As we walk into the club I am about to burst with pride. In the past I had some queens saying I was making him up. Figment of my imagination. My best friend D.D. spit out her gum when she saw us walking in. It was so funny. I ordered my usual, bourbon and diet coke, C.K. ordered a beer. We start the introductions, I knew it would be campy. I warned him on the way. He told me he was a big boy, that he could handle it. Some patrons and some of the queens tried to hit on C.K. I was not worried at all. I told the bartender to watch out for my man, send for me if I needed to come up here and slap a ho! So the show starts, we have an opening production number that included the entire cast, then individual talents. There was a 15 minute intermission, individual talent again, then a full on closing production number. Friday and Saturday night we had 2 shows. So he was going to have to sit through another one if he was going to stay with me until I went home. After the first show, we change into travel drag, so we can make the circuit. All of the bar owners were in good standing with each other. Each had a different scene. One was a sports bar, one was a neighborhood bar, we were the show bar and the last was the one with the exotic male dancers. I liked amateur night there. The guys were not used to dancing on top of the bar, so D.D. and I would place bets on who would fall off! She was so much fun. The girls in the show told me that my man had tipped them all and that his eyes never left me when I was talking or singing on stage. That made my heart smile. So here we are, my best friend, me and my man walking down Bourbon Street. Two queens and a Marine. I loved it. We do the circuit, taking out our compacts in each bar to check our hair and makeup. We wanted to show the up and coming drag children what they should look like. You first have to be a princess, before, one can become a Queen! So many people just flock to drag queens, he didn't seem to mind all of the attention. I hoped he was having a good time. I give him my tips and pay from the first show, as we go backstage to get ready for the 2nd. The second show started at midnight. It was always a little more crazy, the 'go to bed early' tourist were back in their hotels, the 'I have been drinking all day' crowd were out to see the freaks! We always loved the 2nd show. We could be a little more risqué that is as long as we followed Mother Bob's rules. Mother did not play when it came to the shows nor our reputation. Always nails on, pantyhose, plus you had better watch your mouth. My act usually included singing, some comedy and getting to know the audience, as well as emcee. We finished, packed up our stuff and headed home. I was tired, had some appointments in the shop that morning. This was the only day of his visit I could not move the clients to another day. I would be home after 1pm. When we walk into the apartment David and his girlfriend were watching TV popping some corn. We did the hello thing. David had talked to C.K. on the phone for months. He always mailed something to Dave from his military travels. We go upstairs and I start peeling off the layers of drag like a painted up onion. C.K. helps me with the necklace and the zippers. He goes downstairs to visit while I took a shower and got ready for bed. I put on my black silk robe then opened the bathroom door. He was in bed, under the covers to a little above his waist. He had a red rose, a teddy bear, along with two big glasses of water. I sip all night y'all, like a camel. I cry because no one had ever given me flowers before. I was very nervous about us spending the night together. I had already learned that sex was a tool or even a weapon to some. He gets up, hugs me tight, kisses me and we turn out the lights. I have to say that was the most amazing night of my life. I learned the difference between having sex and making love. Love was no longer taboo to me.

The rest of the week was like a new adventure in the city I loved with the man I loved. I saw David bloom and we both were so very happy. On the last night before C.K. was to fly out, we were sad. But we could still hold one another for now. That was a comfort. He told me about how some of the accidents and the accidental killings on base were not so accidental. That Marines were being set up, some not even gay and thrown out. That he had to constantly watch what he said, piss off the wrong person and they could report you. Once they were being watched it was as good as over for that person. He assured me I had nothing to worry about. Some of my friends said he was the butchest fag they had ever met. No one could tell. Unless they found out about me. When he was leaving all I could do was cry. He said Ms. Fifi you have all of my body and my heart. I have the rest of my life to prove it to you. Then those 3 words. Got cab fare? No I kid. I LOVE YOU!! And so did I.

Chapter 11

There was a sickness that had fallen over my community. Some of my friends were sick and the doctors and could not figure out what was wrong with them. One of the bartenders had large dark places appearing on his legs. I had never seen anything like it. Others were losing weight, or could not shake a cold. I was worried. One of the local gay news publications had a story about the new gay cancer. It was showing up in the cities with large gay populations that many of the sick had the same kind of symptoms. Mother Bob came to us during rehearsal, asked if we would mind just doing the show for tips, so she could give the money to an employee who was too sick to work, that his rent was due. We all agreed and the shows went on as usual. I was making plenty of money at the shop, David was still working full time with the landlords, so we were good. There were meetings, government documents put out, oh and every preacher on the planet was calling this God's revenge on the gays. What was the worst, everyone and I mean everyone was dying. It was hitting very close to home. When C.K. would call I would tell him from his last visit, who had died and who was now sick.

As I was becoming successful, we were able to travel more. Mostly I would fly to a state near C.K. rent a room and he would find his way to me. We had to be careful and always met at least 100 miles from the base he was stationed. Our bond grew, was very strong. I loved him with all my heart, I had no doubt he loved me.

We worked out a plan so I could still write letters to him. A very pretty lipstick lesbian friend posed for pictures with C.K. I will call her L.L. At different spots around the city. He had the photos to show to his buddies of his girlfriend. We would mail him a photo of her and I just happened to be in it. That way he always had new pics to show the guys and that would explain why he never went with the girls like they did. He was in love and it was serious. He was saving up to buy a ring. That they were high school sweethearts. Genius if I do say so myself.

C.K. and I planned a trip to Vegas. I was going to fly in the day before him. Check into the Stardust and rent us a car. He flew in from San Diego, took a cab from the airport. We had 4 days and I was not going to waste them. We had bought him some clothes while he was in New Orleans so I packed for both of us. He knocked on the door, I met him in a towel. It was on y'all. I had missed him so very much. He would soon leave for Japan. There was a large base there. He had to go. I would just focus on our 4 days together. We hit every casino, every show, my favorites were watching the volcano erupt and Circus Circus. We laughed, loved and he would hold me at night, all night. I woke up one evening and he was just staring at me. I asked what the hell are you doing. He said how did I get so lucky to have you love me? Melted my heart. He said sometimes he would watch me sleep all night and not sleep himself. How could I not love this man? We were on our last day. Checkout was at 2pm. So we went to breakfast, on the way back to the room, there was this HUGE slot machine. It took 5 dollar coins. We hadn't gambled much so I wanted to play it. I took a 20 to the window, the lady gave me four 5 dollar coins. I would drop in the coin then he would pull the lever. The first 3 were a bust. On the last one we switched, he dropped in the coin, I pulled down the lever. Red, White and then Blue 7's. The slot machine started ringing and flashing. People were looking to see what we had won. We were watching all of these 5 dollar coins drop into the pan. Several casino workers surrounded us, they had these trays for us to fill with the coins. We did and it added up to 1,000 dollars. We were so excited. A lady told me the machine only pays out one thousand, that we would get the rest of our winnings at the window. I was shocked, I was happy with the thousand. We looked on the front of the slot machine to what paid and how much. We found our 7's. 5,000 dollars! I almost fainted. So we collect our winnings, the casino had security escort us to our room. We go in and I start taking off my clothes, he follows my lead. We are all over each other, NAKED, The housekeeper walks out of the bathroom!!!! I was horrified! Embarrassed! I grab the comforter to cover up with. She is as red as a beet. C.K. starts laughing, walks over to the door, penis flopping with each step and opens it for her to leave. Well that killed my mood for sure. He takes 500 dollars for mad money, I am to deposit the rest. We were building our nest egg. The next week he leaves for Japan. I was so worried about him being so far away. He mailed gifts to David and I addressed to L.L. But to my address. He could call once a week.

The Gay Cancer was upgraded to G.R.I.D.S. Gay Related Immune Deficiency Syndrome. We were all doing the shows for free. Even donating our tips. Volunteering to do even more with other queens as often as we could. We were having food drives, along with every holiday we set out a spread in the bars so those who were disowned by their families, were homeless, or couldn't afford the food, all were welcome to come eat with us. The cost of the medicine was astronomical, thousands of dollars a month PER person. Still we were going to do all we could for our community. We were told of other queens and groups doing the same as us in other cities. There were protests starting against the government. I was going to at least 1 funeral a week. Some funeral homes would not even accept the bodies. Hospitals were turning people away. In one year I went to 85 funerals. I was terrified.

Now we hear the word A.I.D.S. Acquired Immune Deficiency Syndrome. Our local gay papers have many stories about this disease. The mainstream papers, if anything it was still all about the gays. The President had not even said the word and when he finally did the amount of money for research and treatment was pathetic. As Julia Sugarbaker said, y'all aren't doing anything because you figure this disease is killing all the right people!! This disease was clearly in other parts of the population, but it was only a gay story. It had gotten to the point we were spending all of our free time and much of our personal income just trying to keep up with the demand within our own community. We were hosting fundraisers almost every day. We decided to rent a banquet hall to do a multi burb event for all in the area to see if we combined our efforts and could raise more money. One friend owned a local car dealership. I asked if it would be possible for us to raffle off a new car. He told me they can donate a car to charity, then it would be a tax write off to cover the dealership, as long as it was below X amount of dollars. We get the car, now let's start selling tickets. Each ticket sold for 50 dollars. With so many communities linked now we had a wonderful response to this, along with other donated items we sold. We had Drag Queen housekeeping, bartenders for parties, chefs to cook in people's homes. Anything we could think of to make a buck. Don't think our working girls were not doing their part as well. The ladies of the evening donated money, time, also helped in people's homes. We moved sick people in together to save on rent, plus we could tend to them more efficiently. We were unified and nothing was going to stop us. The car raffle, silent auctions, services we sold, along with other efforts raised 50 thousand dollars. The person who won the car then sold it and donated that money as well.

There was so much fear and confusion, plus hate flying over the airwaves, TV, radio. All the people in government, religion, TV evangelists were just foaming at the mouth with lies and myths spreading as much hate and fear as possible. Gays have always been the blame for every evil in this nation. Sadly, we know it is still happening today. Right in my very state of Louisiana. In my 20's I did rededicate my life to Christ. I joined a church. I was told I had to testify to the minister, tell my story. He did not keep my words to himself. He told many in the congregation. One woman started the 'I want James out of my church' movement. It worked, people were talking about me like I was a dog. Sad part is I had been doing her hair for years. I swore I would never go to church again.

The temperatures of summer in the Deep South soared. I have always heard it is not the heat that will kill ya, it was the humidity. I was leaving an AIDS rally near Spanish Plaza, it was PRIDE time again. I was excited, C.K. was flying in to see his 'girlfriend' the lesbian. He had not seen the Gay Pride celebration in the Big Easy. Let me tell you, it is a show for sure. In our community we do our best to take care of our own. We party and play, we have to, without being with other people like us, we simply would not make it. We as a community have always managed to laugh through the discrimination. The Church and Right Wing policies had pushed us into the dark, where we developed our culture, now they use this very behavior, which they created against us. Hypocritical to say the least.

So I was walking home, passing through tourist and friends alike. I had not noticed anything out of the ordinary. There were some men following me. I am two blocks from home, someone taps me from behind on my shoulder. I stop and turn, figured it was a sister who wanted to wish me a happy pride, or say hi. It wasn't. This man put his arm around my neck, as if to hug me, in that brief moment I was trying to see who this man was behind those mirrored sunglasses. He said, BURN IN HELL FAGGOT! God and I hate you. Then he shoved a knife deep into my side. It felt like I had been set on fire where the knife went in. He twisted the knife a few times as it was in me. He pulled it out, then hit me in my face. I fell to the ground. I couldn't breathe or scream, I grabbed my side, looked at my hand, it was covered in my blood. Someone asked are you ok? I think they thought I had fallen down, that happens a lot in the French Quarter. She saw the blood and started yelling for help. It happened so fast I really didn't get a good look at any of their faces. The ambulance came, so I was getting the treatment I needed. It didn't take long for the word to get out Fifi had been stabbed. My best friend D.D. went to our apartment to be with David. I did not know that at the time, but, was very happy she did. C.K. arrived on the shuttle, he had his key and just let himself in. D.D. told him what had happened. She later told me he started to shake and ran to the trash can to throw up. That huge tears fell from his silent eyes. She told him what hospital I was in, so he left immediately. I had only seen him cry when we talked about my past. He walked up to the bed I was in at the ER. I have tears now remembering this. He lied to the doctors, said he was my brother so he could get in to see me. There are still places in the country same sex partners are not allowed in a hospital room, we are not family. I know people who have passed away that their partner's family would not let them in, so they died apart. He takes my hand. His is shaking as tears drip from his face. The ER doctor looks at my x-rays, tells me how lucky I was that the blade missed all of my internal organs. That I was going to be, in time, ok. I was so relieved. All I could think about were my two guys. I asked C.K. to please call David so he could stop worrying. He said D.D. was with him. He agreed, but, he didn't let go of my hand. He started to shake more, he was crying, this time out loud. It broke my heart. He looked at me, said I am sorry, I can't let go. He looked at the nurse, then said the same over and over. I can't let go. I can't let go. I started to cry as well, I could not stand to see him in so much pain. The nurse asked would you like me to call. I said yes please, I gave her my number, then told her my brother's name was David. She looked at me, I thought this was your brother David? She said, it's ok. I will call. When she came back into the room, C.K. was sitting in a chair, with his head down, still holding my hand. With a tear in her eyes, she said. One day I hope someone loves me this much. I knew this man, this Marine trained to be tough, well he loved me. In a couple of days the Dr. releases me and I go home. David was so very happy to see me. C.K. was still there, not exactly how we planned his visit to go, but, I had him there. C.K. was doing the cooking, Dave filled me in on every moment of his television shows while I was away. There was an investigation, my attack was reported as a failed robbery attempt. Oh how that still pisses me off. On the last day of his visit, C.K. comes in with a tiny cocker spaniel puppy. She is party color, black and white. We named her Tash, which was a form of Cajun French for the word spot.

Chapter 12

Fifi was back at work in a week, not in a show yet, but in the salon. C.K. and I decided we needed to see more of each other. The time apart was tough on us both, as was all the hiding and secrets. He was being transferred to a base in North Carolina. There were beaches nearby and summer rentals. I planned on taking David for vacation, but, now I had many medical bills to pay. For some reason I am having panic issues when I am out in public and was always scared.

The charity work was going well, we were traveling to more cities all over the country. Doing as many benefits and fund raisers as we could. Our national community had banded together to help one another. We had to, no one else was. Celebrities along with other public figures were on board in the fight against this horrible disease. After two years of a week here, a week there, keeping up with my hair clients, doing shows, I was starting to feel exhausted. C.K. was deployed overseas. He called it the Storm. I was terrified for him. I was still working with hospice, group homes, all the queens were still organizing benefits. We were feeding people, paying electricity bills, rent for others, even dog walking if needed. The people who passed away many had pets. So we found them safe homes as well. I would get a letter of card from C.K. from time to time. Still addressed to L.L. I was swamped at the shop. I had more people trying to make appointments than I could handle. Booking me at least 6 weeks in advance. The attitude toward gay people was at an all-time low. Two of my inner circle friends were murdered. No one was ever caught. I wondered if they had even looked. There were so many church groups that would come into the French Quarter, stand outside our bars and beg God to destroy us. I have seen the patterns in my life, preachers with power will condemn us and then someone on the fringe of this ideology would act out against us. Target us. I was worried about David being by himself so much.

I asked David if he wanted to go with me to Biloxi, we had not been before on my two days off. He said yes. We stayed at the Biloxi Beach Resort. Loved this place, it was like stepping back in time. Cute retro rooms. Had an amazing pool, bar, restaurant at a very affordable price. Walk across HWY 90 and you were on the beach. We took a tour out to Ship Island. I fell in love with the oceanarium. Then bingo!! I found a fabulous little gay club. Just Us! Was painted all in jungle scenes. Friendly laid back people. I knew the first day I wanted to move. Fifi didn't make this trip, but, she would the next one. Once we were back in the Quarter, we were rested and relaxed. Possibly hung over as well. I asked David to give his two week notice with our landlords. I still didn't like him walking to the complexes alone. I see now I was already paranoid. He had no problem with it, took to the life of leisure right away. It was such a relief to me. The shows were still popular, especially with the tourist. For me the entire mood had changed. With so many friends dead or dying and my attack. I had lost some of my love for this special city, once I had blead on its streets. We still had Tea Dance at the Pub, I remember the day OZ opened. We Pubettes said it would never last. We were wrong. Every weekend and major holiday, there was this one religious group that would come. Oh they made me furious. They had one member who would dress in Jesus drag. Remember, you are born naked, everything else is drag. Anyway he would put on a plastic crown to thorns. Then drag this HUGE Styrofoam cross that had wheels on it, in front of our bars. The megaphone screaming I did not die for you to live like this. You all are abominations before God. There were many more as well. I was tired of it! My friend D.D. was attacked on North Rampart Street, just two minutes after I had passed. We were in drag. The men who kicked and beat her quoted bible verses the entire time. I had noticed more anger growing against my community. Most of it was religious or politically motivated. As the good people of America did nothing we were being terrorized. I honestly believe when Harvey Milk was assassinated. The legal team used the Twinkie, gay panic defense for the killer. It worked he got away with murder. Then committed suicide. The tone was set. Even the queen who started the Stonewall Riots Martha P. Washington was found murdered a few years later. If the gays get too much power, too out, or too proud, shut them up by any means needed. The law was against us. I myself had been arrested for not having the legal number of men's garments on to be in public as a female impersonator. We had spotters outside the bars, so if we were going to be raided and we were, we could have time to switch dancing partners because it was illegal for two men to dance together. The spotters were not always right and yes I was arrested once for slow dancing with another man. I had policemen call me names and spit on me many times. Even at the small club that was in Monroe, we would call the police to remove the people who stood in the streets wanting to hurt us as we went to our cars. Sometimes, an officer would join them. We were losing our jobs, homes and lives.

So over a year has passed since C.K. had been deployed, he was back in North Carolina. I plan the trip for Dave, Tash and me. We had a car now. A yellow Subaru GL10. It was so cute. Had the fake wooden panels on the outside. Like a WOODIE, a sunroof and a computer dash board. If I would have known what was to come I would have just went back in the apartment and locked the door. It was a very long drive. Tash was beautiful, freshly groomed and loved riding in the car. She loved her Uncle David, Dad who was C.K. and Mommy, me. David was excited to be going on a road trip. I wanted to see my man. As we were driving down these little winding roads and small towns I felt my stress levels drop. There was no navigation then. We did have flip phones that were 5 dollars a minute when in roam, printed directions from a computer and printer the size of a double oven! We stop along the way, Tash on her leash, me needing to pee every 200 miles. I can't get 50 now. The last stop for gas before the end of our journey was in a small town named, Sneads Ferry. I felt very uneasy with the men standing outside the service station with their hunting rifles. David took the money in for the gas and I would have rather peed in my pants than ask for the restroom. We cross a small bridge and then we see the Atlantic! Oh it was beautiful. Did not look the same as the Gulf. Was much bluer. We checked into our rental, unpacked, then took Tash out for a walk. She was scared of the crabs on the beach. Honestly I was too. She barked at the sea gulls. Just one or two barks at a time. She wasn't very talkative. Just enough to get me to notice what she was telling me. We saw jellyfish on the shore. Some looked very strange, we later learned those were man o' war and to avoid them. David pointed out wild dolphins and I was ready to see C.K. He had been wounded during his deployment, we had talked and he said he was fine. I just had to see him with my own eyes. I didn't pick him up. We thought it was best he came in a cab at night as not to be so easily seen. We kept the blinds closed, so he could stay hidden. He not once got to go to the beach with us. I look back and it was all just so wrong. We had to hide for 20 years. David would walk Tash for me. I kept remembering his words, the suspected gay people met an ugly fate.

The first few weeks were amazing. When C.K. could visit we would stay in. I would cook, all of us would play board games. I always lost. The times he was away I would lay out, my tan was AMAZING. Thought I would need Black Lady Foundation. The island has a small grocery store that had everything we needed. C.K. had to change his plans to visit, we had a hurricane coming. Bertha. Now Dave and I had experienced some storms. We had Andrew and a few other blow through New Orleans. Bertha wasn't very strong, so we were not worried.

The storm hits, no big deal, we schedule a visit the coming weekend. I was getting cabin fever. So I read in the little paper a local bar was going to have Karaoke. This was the new thing and it was hot. Being a singer I figured if I entertained the locals they would not kill me. The people in the grocery store and the ones I had met on the beach seemed nice enough. I didn't bring any drag with me...was going to be all James. I walk to the bar and just a few blocks away was beachfront. It is the cutest place. Built and decorated to resemble a ship. Very good woodwork on the inside. Beautiful wooden bar with the barstools made to look like Captains wheels. There are people at both ends of the bar and a fair amount of empty space in the middle. So I pick my spot then settle in. No murse this trip either. I used my pockets. The bartender was a very pretty young lady with HUGE boobs. I ordered a drink and she asked if I was a member. No, do I have to be? Yes she answered, but, I can sell you a one day membership for 5 dollars. I said well sign me up! She asked for my ID. Saw I was from New Orleans she handed me a slip, I signed it, gave her the money and there was my drink. She asked why I was there. I said my brother and I were on vacation. Do you like it here? I had to say yes, it was such a nice place and I had never been on an island before. She told me to keep the membership card and that if I wanted to come back or go to another bar just show it and pay the 5 dollars again. So she tends to the other patrons and I am just chilling with my bourbon. I have a few drinks in me when the karaoke people come in to set up. She asked me if I sang. Yes I do. She brought me a book, some paper slips and a pencil. I thumb through, pick out a couple I think the crowd will like, then turn them in. A few people sing, then I hear next up is James. I did Statue of a Fool. Nailed it. Nice applause from the people, someone sent me a drink. I thanked them and listened to what sounded like a woman skinning a cat, to a Judd's song. I ordered a lemon drop and another drink. About an hour later I hear my name again. This time I do, At This Moment. They loved it. This time someone sent a dink and a shot. The bartender came over, you could be a professional singer. I laughed, said thank you, but, I would stick to the bar circuit. Two men came over, shook my hand and asked me a couple questions. I said I was a hair stylist from New Orleans. They quickly ended the conversation. Not in a mean way, just wanted to get away from me. I was starting to get uncomfortable as there were many more people coming in and some were really drinking heavily. I pay my check, tip a 20 and am ready to go. The bartender says in a very low tone. Do not go to this bar in Jacksonville. It is gay and it is being watched. I was shocked. I didn't know what she meant but I sure was going to find out.

Chapter 13

The next night I get ready, call a cab and then head to Jacksonville. I was surprised at how large the town was. We drive up to the bar, I pay the cab fare and step out. It was only about a 30 minute cab ride, not too far from where we were staying. The place was pretty full. I could tell some were military, had a nice mix of men and women. I sit at the bar, take my "membership card" out and show it to the bartender. He was a hoot! Wearing a Speedo, high heels and a rubber swimming cap with multi colored flowers, he asked me if I was single because I had a nice package. I said thank you, but I was in a L.T.R. He looked at the card and laughed. Mary you don't need that here. I clocked you the second you walked through the door. You my dear are family. I was thrilled knowing I could relax and be me. I tell him what was said to me on the island the night before. He exclaimed, oh hell yes honey they are watching. Astonishingly he went on to say, thanks to Jesse Helms, the local Christian radio stations, the churches and half of our fucking congress, we were ordered to turn over all of our "membership cards" so they could pursue their goddamn witch hunt of our customers then they would turn their names over to the fucking Marines. I thought about C.K. and my heart skipped a beat. I hesitantly asked, already knowing the answer, will they be in trouble. He replied, MARY they will be thrown out of the military, lose their pensions and have a dishonorable discharge. I said that truly was horrible, not having the words to express my disgust. He says, getting a bit 'flamed up' this fucking state don't care…goddamn bible beaters. Expressing my own frustration by saying, well I guess it's ok to die for your country as long as you're in the closet. His salty answer…Fucking Ehh! He said well, we fucking showed them assholes. We drove all of the membership cards we had right to the fucking front gate of the base. The bar owner poured gas on them and we set them ablaze! He defiantly laughed out loud. That the flames he described almost matched his own made me smile…she was a flamer. He told me about gay people's houses in the area being burned down, that someone had climbed onto the roof of the bar, used a shotgun to shoot holes in it while they were open for business with people inside and that 19 lesbians have been fucking raped and that there had been several recent murders and that even the owner of this bar had been attacked and stabbed several times. One attack, the knife went through his eye and became lodged in the roof of his mouth. That the guy tried and couldn't pull it back out was sickening and I was overcome with grief and anger. I asked, is he buried near here? I was going to take some flowers to his grave. Oh naw MARY, he didn't fucking die, you will see that lucky son of a bitch in the fucking drag show at 10! I was amazed, I had to meet this queen and she had to come to New Orleans to tell her story. As I expected the show was great. The courage and bravery these people were showing inspired me. After talking to the queens who were in the show, I hear multiple horror stories. LGBT people were being run off the roads in their vehicles, stalked and beaten up in public in broad daylight. The police were seemingly not doing a thing. They showed me newspaper clippings from Senator Helms that made my blood boil. It always happens, these people spew their ignorant hate and we as a community suffer from it. It still goes on today. The owner took me into his office to talk. I told him about my attacks and he was moved to ask me if I feel as if I don't want to get out of bed sometimes? Are you scared he asked? I answered yes to both. We hugged as only two survivors could. It is getting close to closing time, they call for a taxi and I hug necks and exchange phone numbers. Then back to the Island. The next morning C.K. calls. Another training accident had happened. Poor guy was shot in the back of the head. They were not even using live rounds, so it was a mystery. It was rumored he was gay. I told him where I had gone earlier and what I had learned. He wasn't happy at all. He said soldiers had been discharged just for going there and that some of the locals and even the M.P.'s were watching to see who comes and goes and that he had never even been and for me not to go back, please. He wanted us to leave because there was another storm brewing. Fran. They were saying it was going to be a bad one. I watched the weather channel and Fran was supposed to hit further south and if it did we would be driving straight into it plus I wanted to see him one more time. I went back to the ship bar a few nights later, it was pretty much empty. Only seven or eight people. Saw the same bartender and she was good because my drink was on the bar before I even sat down. We were laughing and having a good ole time. I asked if she had warned me about the bar in Jacksonville because she thought I was gay. She said James, that stuffed deer head over there on the wall knows you are gay, I just didn't want you to get hurt. Besides, you are a good tipper. We laughed and went on with our evening. It was a short walk to the rental, there were still only a few people there so we cut up and had a great time. She still calls me to this day. Was getting close to closing time, I paid up, tipped her real good, got a hug and walked out. The breeze off of the Atlantic was wonderful. I loved the smell of the air coming from the ocean and it definitely keeps it cooler outside. I was walking along the beach and I hear HEY FAGGOT! As I turn I suddenly see a blade coming at my face. I threw my arm up, the blade sliced from my elbow to my wrist. Another man hit me from behind on the back of my head. It had to have been with some sort of an object, I saw stars. Everything after that was a blur. I remember being stabbed more than once and someone was quoting Leviticus as another was kicking me in my stomach and face. Basically getting my ass beat! My first memory of the attack came the next afternoon. My picture was in the paper describing me as an admitted homosexual and I was 'allegedly' attacked. If you ask I can describe exactly what "allegedly" feels like. There was no police report written even though there were 911 calls made that night. The chief of police was allegedly (that word again) trying to talk to the officers who responded to find out why they didn't make a report. No reasonable answer to that question ever surfaced. Any chance of catching these men was long gone as they had way too much time to get away. The chief asked me if I did this to myself. Blank stare. I could not believe my ears. I answered as best I could without sounding ridiculous…um…no! Why the hell would I? He had talked to the bartender, she said I had left the bar alone, as I had. All I remembered was a man with a baseball cap, his hair was pulled like a pony tail out the back of the hat. Well, obviously I am not traveling for some time to come. I was so happy David and Tash were there with me. C.K. took the news hard. He couldn't come see me but we could talk on the phone. If he had been seen they would have would have figured us out. Once again I am full of rage. He said there were Marines talking about what happened to me on base and they said that it had to be locals. Not being able to react to them saying it was 'because they would have killed the cocksucker' must have been hard for C.K. Fran did hit and it was horrible. I was still meeting with the chief of police getting more and more frustrated. As I recovered, someone painted a swastika along with the words DIE FAG on my front door. They also left a knife with MY dried blood on it in the middle of my welcome mat. Slightly ironic. I staged a 1 man silent protest at the police station. This is where the good American people threw eggs and rocks at me. Nothing was done. They cursed me, condemned me to hell and drove by screaming foul names at me. Even one of the police officers walked out of the station, pulled his gun out and pointed it at me. This is what he said. "If you want to do this in my front yard imagine what I can do in yours." That was it. I didn't care if I was well enough to drive or not. My family was the getting the hell out of there. We drove back to New Orleans. I was scared all of the time and I learned some new words. Post Traumatic Stress Disorder or P.T.S.D. We do our best to try to get on with life moving forward. At that time I was back working in the beauty shop and just starting to do some shows but due to my injuries I had to sit on the stage to sing. A few months go by, I am getting my groove back. As things go in my life, I suffer another blow. Mother Bob passes away. My drag mother. There were apartments above the bar. She and her longtime partner of 40 years live in one, my friend D.D lived in another. I never will forget the day of her funeral. We were all to meet at her bar, there was a jazz band and we were dressed in our finest drag. I was wearing a smart little black dress, size 6, black pantyhose and a very sensible 4" heel. Also in my favorite black wig and a simple pearl necklace Mother Bob had given me when I won my first pageant. We had her ashes along with permission to throw them into the Mississippi River as long as they were in a special sealed container. The band starts playing Just a Closer Walk with Thee. The slow march from North Rampart St. to the Mississippi begins. If you have not seen a jazz funeral live I can't explain the emotion nor the sendoff your loved one gets. We have our beaded, feathered umbrellas. The march is step slide step slide. Everyone stops as we pass in the Quarter, having a large pack of Drag Queens, Lesbians, Queers and Trans people we were a sight to see. As we work our way to the final destination no one talks. We are quiet unless singing with the band. It is an unwritten rule where ladies touch the pearls and gentlemen tip their hats as we pass by. During this part we are mourning the loss of our loved one. Feeling our sadness. It was 12 blocks to the river and with the slow pace it takes a while to get there. Once we are all arranged on the steps leading to the muddy water the band starts playing Amazing Grace. As we all sing to honor Mother Bob it was so emotional. This person took me in as her own, fed me when I was hungry, held me when I cried, made me feel like a person again. The band stops playing once we finish the song. D.D. takes the box to the water's edge. She said to Mother how she will be missed but never forgotten. Then she throws it into the water. It goes under for two seconds then pops right back up to the surface. I was horrified. I wasn't swimming out there to get her. It sinks and comes back up again! The third time it did sink then D.D. said and I quote "Well that is the first time in that old bitch's life she didn't just go down!" We all laugh through our tears. We hug her partner and at that moment the band strikes up with When the Saints Go Marching In as it could only be played in New Orleans. Now we are to celebrate knowing this person and their life. Laughter, high stepping and flinging our beaded and feathered umbrellas in the blue summer sky. The route back now that is a different story. There are many stops, at many bars. We were not B drinking today. We were going to party. Complete strangers join in the festivities, as they should. This is all a part of life. A celebration. We all know we will not live forever. We were carrying our heels by the time we made it back to Mother Bob's bar. As sad as I was, I have to tell y'all. It was one of the most amazing days of my life. To have a family of friends, well to me, was a hell of a lot better than the one I was born into. I would say about three months later I was working in the shop, David calls me, something was wrong. His girlfriend had died. I rush home. She was found in her apartment and it seemed from natural causes. I felt so bad for him. He was devastated. We learned after the autopsy she died from liver disease. She was so sweet to David, I loved her like she was my sister. I just knew they were going to get married. Dave has not had a serious girlfriend since. He has had girlfriends y'all. I just think this scarred him for life. It took years for him to go out on another date. We paid for her funeral, there was no family to claim her. David said he would pay me back. I told him it was our money, not mine, so don't worry about it at all. I hated to see him hurting. I was about to suffer a loss myself. One that would change me forever. Two of the original people I had met when I first started working in the motel. The very queen that loaned me her Rusted Rhinestone necklace. Well her boyfriend of 30 years had been sick with Aids. They had moved into a small apartment just outside of the French Quarter in the Faubourg Marigny area about a year after we left the motel. I saw them all of the time. We would have dinner parties and go to Mardi Gras parades together. I did their hair at the shop for free. I could not charge my family. I loved them. She called to say he was gone and asked me to you please come over. I dropped everything and did just that as it was only a few blocks away. Some other friends were there already and I was the last to arrive. He was in their bed when he had passed away. She had cleaned him up and dressed him in a tuxedo. His makeup well, let's just say, a funeral home could not have done any better. The tux was dated, from the 70's with big ruffles but he still looked handsome. She had a wedding dress hanging on the door, I had seen it a million times in her apartment. Just waiting for the day it would be legal. They were so bonded in life. We all feared she was going to take her own life as she could not go on without him. Y'all gay life is tough. Imagine all they had been through? We were just now gaining some social approval. My heart was breaking. Even with the changes that had come, it doesn't take away the hurt caused by the past. I knew this first hand. She wanted me to fix her wig and the others to paint her face. She said we couldn't be married in this life, so we will be ready in the next. We all agreed to do as she asked. How could we not? Still, daily, we were blasted by religion, government and law. She had pills and took them. I was working on her wig. She kept changing how she wanted it styled. With tears in my eyes I asked, BITCH did you take enough pills? And when will they work? We all laughed. She walked over to me, gave me a hug and a kiss. She said Fifi I claim you as my daughter. Then gave me the necklace. Said it is yours now. I still have it to this day. She was passing on instructions about her makeup. I joked with her again. Gurl we need a staple gun to get that look on your face. Everyone laughs again. She told us all how very dear we were to them. Then put on the dress. It all happened faster than I thought it would. She laid down next to him. Went to sleep and soon enough she was gone. We did as she wished, looked at them side by side. She in her wedding dress, him in his tux. Was a beautiful sight and a sad one as well. I had lost two people I loved. Their hospice worker called the police when she arrived.

I knew we had to move soon. The city I had so loved now had too many memories of death and violence. I asked God. Why am I still here? Why didn't I die? It wasn't that people had not tried to kill me. What was my purpose? I drove to Biloxi the next weekend to start looking for a condo. Didn't take long, it was perfect. Right across from the beach, 2 bedroom 2 bath. Each bedroom had a huge balcony with sliding glass doors. In the living room it had floor to ceiling glass overlooking the beautifully landscaped pool. I could touch the palm tree off of my bedroom balcony. The living area, kitchen, dining were completely open concept, one large room. It was so much bigger than what we were used to. Not 50 yards away was the perfect place for a beauty shop. David and I pack up, then hit the road. The yellow Subaru was not my thing anymore. Traded it in on an Infinity M30 convertible. Oh it was pretty. Black with a black top and gray leather interior. We were accepted by the locals, had no problems at all. Was hoping my luck had changed. C.K. would fly into New Orleans, I would pick him up. He loved the condo and we were a very happy yet unconventional family.

Chapter 14

Everything was smooth sailing, shop was doing great and Fifi was doing shows in New Orleans and Biloxi. I forgot to tell y'all her back story. Fifi Frost was the illegitimate love child of Jack Frost and Mrs. Claus. Because Santa only comes once a year!! C.K. and I had been building our savings, I figured we were in the perfect spot to retire when the time came. I could keep the shop, rent out the booths, if I wanted, still do some clients from time to time. Over the next few years we went on a few cruises, I was doing shows in New York, Dallas and Key West. I had started speaking at events focused on equality, rights and yes, my attacks. I was seeing a therapist because I was having severe headaches and trouble sleeping because so many memories from my life came back to haunt me. There were days I could not even get out of bed. My dreams were nightmares. My dentist had me wear a mouth guard because I was constantly grinding my teeth. C.K. and I plan a getaway. Hot Springs Arkansas, I love it there. I flew in on the 10th of September 2001. He was going to meet me on the 12th. I was so excited to see him. We were staying at the Arlington Hotel for some much needed pampering and R & R. The lobby was a vision of days gone by. Grand and opulent. A wonderful bar on the right side of the lobby as you walk in, bandstand on the left. Surrounded by incredible murals on the walls. They still hosted ball room dancing. I loved to see the ladies glide across the floor in their gowns. Next door was the Park Hotel with a quaint little open air cocktail lounge and an Italian Restaurant to die for. Both were completely tiled in mosaics. Floors and walls. On the 11th I was scheduled for an early morning massage then mineral water treatments. I was wearing, for the first time, my long silk robe C.K. had sent me from his time in Japan. Oh it was beautiful. Gold silk with embroidered dragons and coy fish. It was a vision of old Hollywood glamor. The colors were vivid and it would flow behind me when I walked. Add some fab gold slippers with a tiny kitten heel and I was ready for my close up. I was a vision of perfect masculinity. The elevator doors open, I take a quick step exiting to start the effect of the flow. Another guest walks to me and said. Did you hear what happened? I thought to myself. They had better not have closed the spa! No ma'am what? They attacked us she said. Who attacked us I asked? She said we don't know, but, they flew a jet into the World Trade Center. I gasp wanting to know more. The staff were setting up a large projection television on the band stand so I walked over to see. They turned it on, I was horrified. I saw footage of the first plane crashing into the tower. As I sat there watching a second jet flew into the other tower. Everyone screamed. I could not believe my eyes. I could not move. A waitress from the restaurant asked if I wanted to order some breakfast or coffee. I asked if the bar was open. She answered it could be, what would you like? A Bloody Mary please, heavy on the Mary, light on the bloody. The reporter on the television said all air space was closed along with all federal buildings that were being evacuated. The lady brought me my drink, said that the V.A. Hospital was being evacuated up the street and that some of the people would be coming to the hotel then she asked my room number to charge the drink to. The couple next door kept me up all night fighting so I gave her their room number. They owed me this much. All flights were grounded. C.K. was not coming! I thought about David, Tash, C.K. and all my friends in New Orleans. There is a World Trade Center there too. I weep for the people I see jumping out of the buildings and for all involved. The rescue people, police, firefighters and their families as well. The story changes, a jet hit The Pentagon, another crashed in a field somewhere. I could not take it all in. It was completely overwhelming. I am not good at quiet tears, I finished my drink quickly then hurried to my room. I put my face in the pillow and let the screams begin. I needed to hear from everyone NOW. I knew our military was going to have to do something. I wanted them to. I pull myself together, call David. He is watching. We say our I love you's and be safe. I told him I would be home as soon as I could. He was cool with that. I couldn't call C.K. so I had to wait until he called me. That really scared me. I could not call because some people didn't want people like him in the military. That someone may find out about me. I was pissed all over again. I pulled the drawer out in the nightstand to find the phone book. I needed a tattoo parlor open NOW. I wanted to get a tat to show my support for our military, my man and my country. I call several, find one that is going to stay open. I dressed and hailed a cab. Met with the artist. I wanted God Bless America, the flag blowing in the wind, red, white and blue. And some stars.

He sketches a few things until I see something I like. He told me he could do it in one sitting and for this kind of custom work it would be 600 dollars. I asked you take visa? He said yes, I said get to work. It took all day and his work was amazing. The receptionist called a local news team, they sent a reporter, with a camera man. A quick interview and once again I was on the news. I treated everyone in the shop to lunch while he was working on my arm. While we were watching the television we saw the towers fall one by one. Everyone was so emotional and even with all my gasps watching the news unfold before our eyes he never made a mistake. When he finished and my arm was wrapped in cling wrap. I hugged everyone and took a cab back to the hotel. I went to the bar, ordered a bourbon and Diet Coke. I guess it cut down on the calories. I always said diet until I tried it with water and liked that even better. Sorry I strayed. The lobby was full of people. Some were crying. There was a minister there praying with people, talking with them and providing comfort. For the circumstances I thought it was very fitting and needed. When he walked over to me sitting at the bar he asked would you like to pray. I answered politely, no sir, right now I just need to hear from my family, but thank you. The bartender pointed out my new tattoo. It is right beside a very obvious one of the double male symbol, all done in the rainbow ink. He pointed to the double male tat. He asked what does this one mean. I answered it represents my partner who was in the Marine Corps. He said Partner? I said lover. He looked me dead in the eye and said. Good luck getting into heaven. I just said God bless you sir. He couldn't resist the jab. My cell finally rings, it is C.K. and he was angry. His cousin was in tower 2. So this just got a lot closer to home. He had told his family about us years ago. He was already a Marine, so there was no kicking him out of the house. They did kick him out of their lives though. We never saw them the entire time we were together. He wanted me to get home. He said rent a car, I told him I was on my forth drink. He laughed, said quit drinking, sleep and rent one in the morning. He asked if I had heard from David. I told him yes and we were all fine. I send him a pic of the tat. He said thank you for doing that from him and his buddies. Then the I love you's and he hung up. There were people going out to shop, laughing, like nothing had happened. I know people handle situations differently, I just didn't understand joy on 9/11/01! I did rent a car the next morning and drive myself home. Was good to see

David and Tash. Work was nothing except talking about the attacks. The stylists knew him and about us. It was so nice to have them ask about C.K. I wondered if we went to war, how I would hear from him. I would pray that God would keep him safe.

Chapter 15

My therapist was still working with me and my P.T.S.D. We were trying medications. All the wrong medications but he said it was the process of elimination. Still made me bat shit crazy! I was drinking and smoking more than I had ever in the past. I thought about mom. I knew a change was going to have to come.

We hadn't heard anything from dad. We did keep in touch with his sister. She called and asked if we could come visit the coming weekend. There was something we needed to talk about. I asked what is up. She said it was better to do it in person. Ok we will be there. I move my appointments around and tell Dave we will be going then finish out the week. I wondered if someone was sick, hurt, or what was wrong? We drive up to her house around 3:00 in the afternoon. We did our hugs, hello's, she loved the Infinity. We walk in and there sat dad on her sofa. Looking older, but, dad. He thanked us for coming, asked us to sit. I know he could tell by the look on my face I was not happy to see him. He starts talking. He wanted to divorce the step mother. The woman he wanted to be seeing would not let him until he filed for divorce. The stepmother would not sign the papers unless David and I signed everything over to her. Our entire inheritance. She would keep the house, land, everything. We didn't get anything when mom died. I had already told dad years ago, that whatever he was going to leave to me I didn't want it. Give it to David. That he wasn't my father, he was just the cock I rode in on. I was done with it. I told David it was his call. David asked dad. Will this make you happy? Dad said yes. Dave said ok then let's do it. Looked at me, James can we go home now? I said not till we sign the papers. Dad had them and the notary came over. It was final. We drive home. The next news from our aunt was that dad had moved in with his brother and was right down the street from his new sweetheart. David did not speak of dad again for a very long time. That was fine with me. The ex-stepmother told my aunt she couldn't believe dad cheated on her. I laughed. I thought BITCH how did you meet him? Karma!!

The announcement is made. We are going to war in Afghanistan. I knew C.K. would be sent. He was coming to see me before he was deployed. I was very happy about that. As his arrival date approached I was feeling more like my old self. Any sudden noise like thunder or an engine etc. would make me jump and I had started breaking out into sweats and shaking. I went to get groceries and bought everything we could possibly need for the visit. We were not even going to leave the condo. He wasn't getting out of my sight. There were people protesting against *Don't Ask Don't Tell* and as soon as he left I was going to be one of them. I was pissed the country he was fighting for and had fought for, may I add been wounded for, was so petty that him loving me would get him thrown out of the service. The news once again was full of McCain and preachers saying the military would stop to function if gays were allowed in. Hey ASSHOLE'S. We are already there. Always have been.

When I am at the airport in New Orleans, I felt a calm come over me. I had a surprise for C.K. if he was up to it. There he was, I see him before he sees me. I catch his eye. The smile that spread across his face was heartwarming. He ran up to me. Dropped his duffle. Just hugged me. He whispered in my ear. Baby it is so good to see you. I asked if he needed to sleep or eat. He said no that he was ok. We get in the car. Kiss until my lips hurt. I put the top down and off we go. So I drive us to my favorite tattoo parlor in Biloxi. We are gonna get tatted up. I had already drawn what I wanted. An eagle with the flag blowing. This time on a pole, with the words God Bless our Troops. He loved it. He surprised me. On the inside of his upper lip, he had them write Fifi. I cried. It had to have hurt. He said now I can kiss you even when you are not around. We had an incredible time. He had gifts for David he had bought on base in California. Now as I write I cry. He gave Dave a card. Told him not to open it until he was gone. When we did open it there were 4 words. I love you brother. He still has it. In the blink of an eye it was time for him to leave. As I watched his plane fly away, I sat and cried. I didn't know when or if I would see him again.

Well it seemed like the father drama was never going to end. He was sick. Bone cancer. He had spoken to a family friend when he found out. He told her I know my boys hate me for all that has happened. She said no they don't and that he had two great sons and he should be proud. I thought honey speak for yourself on that one.

She calls because dad is in ICU. That she thinks we really should come. This might be the end. I talk to Dave, he says lets go. Once again I divide my clients among the girls at work and we leave the next morning. The V.A. Hospital is in Alexandria, Louisiana. As I drive I am thinking of what I am going to say. Well dad it couldn't have been heart trouble. You don't have one of those. Or bone cancer? Well it's not in your backbone, you never had one of those either! But as the miles grew shorter all I really want to do is give him a hug. If he was going to pass away, he deserved some peace. Find a parking spot, we go in. The nurse takes us into the I.C.U. There he was. Frail, sick and old. His eyes lit up when he saw us. He motioned to the nurse. Yes Mr. Swift? Dad said. You see my youngest son standing there? She said yes sir, they both are handsome men. Dad said if there is any plug that can be pulled and make me die, keep him the hell away from it please! She laughed, I did too. Old fart! She leaves and we sit for a talk. I asked if he needed anything. Was he comfortable? He said he was fine. Should I fluff his pillow? He said stay the hell away from my pillows and laughed again. I was joking with my father. It had been over 20 years since I had done that. To me it seemed like mom at the end he was just going to give up. That all he wanted to do was say he was sorry. I would accept an apology. The doctor comes in and we talked. I told dad that I had taught David how to drive and that we would be coming to see him more. Dad was so proud he even shed a tear. I told him, dad I never gave up on Dave. He got his diploma, he drives, and he works with me in the shop. We were happy. Visiting hours were over so we check into a motel for the night. Walk to subway to get supper. As we are driving back the next morning David asks, James can we go home now? I answered not yet, but soon. When we are brought into the I.C.U. Dad was sitting up, his color was returning and he was even feeding himself. His doctors were thrilled and in a few weeks he was released and back living with his brother. He still had cancer, but, it was like he had found a new reason to live. He just needed to know we didn't hate him.

I am happy to say C.K. gets to call more than I ever imagined he would. He was still in Afghanistan, but, some of them were being moved to Iraq. Iraq I asked? Why? He didn't have an answer and this was before GW told us about going there. He was in good spirits and he had even told a fellow Marine about us. That was after he admitted to him that he had a partner too. I was so happy he had someone to talk to that he could trust. Keeping everything inside was very hard on him. I just wanted him home with me. As the death toll would rise, I would hear on the news more U.S. soldiers were killed. I would pray, please send an Angel to the soldiers and one to their families. There was so much loss, pain, worry and sadness. The next time he calls I am so happy to see that crazy number show up on my phone. He asked me to please go to all the army surplus stores, buy all of the Kevlar, body armor, anything for them to put on. That they were in unarmored Humvees and had NO body protection at all. NOTHING!! He told me that they were raiding the junked vehicles, finding whatever they could to help them. He paused, they were pulling a door off a shot up Humvee and 3 fingers from a fallen Marine fell out of it. My blood ran cold. He told me where to take the armor and the address for it to be sent. I was FURIOUS! How dare you GW, Cheney and Rumsfeld! That comment: "Well you don't fight a war with the perfect Army, you fight it with the one you have." I will NEVER forgive these war criminals for as long as I live. I put the calls out to everyone I knew. Buy it and send it to me, I would wire them the money. Every piece of body armor in 3 states is now on a cargo plane to Iraq. Seven thousand dollars' worth. I would have bought more if we could have found it! SHAME ON YOU Cheney, GW, Rumsfeld! The last thing he said I will remember for the rest of my life. He said, baby they lied to us. I will never trust our government again. Then GW comes on the television. We are going into Iraq!

I get a letter in the mail from California. Addressed to me with no return address. I could tell it was a letter. I open it and start read. Hello James and David. I hope this finds you well. I am not sure how to say this, so here goes. I think I am your sister. I almost fainted! What in the gay hell is this? The letter reads on. When your father lived in California, before he was with my mom. He was seeing a lady there. She got pregnant. Thus the sister. Then dad abandoned them, came back to Louisiana. Took up with our mom. How many lives can one man crush I thought? She had heard he was sick and she wanted to meet him just one time before he passed. I called the Aunt and told her to sit down and spike her prune juice cause she was gonna need it. I read her the letter. All I could hear from her was, Oh lord- Oh Jesus-Oh my goodness as I finished it. She said well, it may be true and that she had heard stories of a baby in

California. But dad said it wasn't his. She had also sent photos. There was one of dad holding her as a baby with her mother standing right by his side. There was no question that was him. She sent one of herself. She looked just like my aunt's on dad's side of the family. I have to go see dad. This time I would go alone. I read him the letter and he denies everything. He asks me James, what are you going to do? I answered dad I have no idea. I have to think about this. We hug and I drive back to Biloxi. Without me knowing my aunt calls another one of the brothers. I have met him tops 3 times in my life and all when I was very young. He steps in and takes over. Dad gets worse and goes back in the hospital. I call and ask if we need to come, he said no and that he was just feeling bad and that his sister would keep us posted. Our uncle makes a trip to see dad. While dad was in the hospital my uncle has him sign power of attorney over to him. I, to this day, will never understand why. My uncle orders a D.N.A. test for the sister in question. She is indeed our sister. Dad is moved into a nursing home when he leaves the hospital. Remember, I know nothing about any of this. Then he uses dad's money to buy her a round trip air plane ticket from California and he pays himself to come in from Denver three separate times. He takes her to the nursing home to meet dad and he also videotaped the meeting. Dad did not speak one word the entire time they were there. When I saw the videotape to me dad looked like he did the night mom was beating us and he stared at a television that wasn't even on. Just a blank, empty stare. When my aunt told me about the things our uncle did well, I called him. Left a message that was not very nice. I told him to get a hobby and stay the fuck out of our lives!! Dad didn't speak again and soon died. I get the call dad has passed and I hated to have to tell David. We pack and start our drive to the funeral home. The uncle uses dad's money once again to fly in the half-sister, as well as himself. We arrive, park and go inside. I meet her in the lobby. We sit to talk it's obvious she is sad and I didn't know what to say. I wanted to tell her she was better of not knowing him when the uncle walks up as we are talking. In the spirit of keeping the peace I offer an apology for my call. He said not accepted and that there was no excuse then walked away. What an asshole!! The new sister didn't like that at all. I said don't worry about it that with this family I am use to it. I walked in to see dad. What he had told David and me about his funeral and wanting it to be like moms, as cheap as possible, was not what happened. THOUSANDS of dollars went to this day. I was disgusted. He did look good though. A little too much rouge for my taste. Another uncle was sitting near the casket. The 'blew her brains out' uncle said, I will not tolerate you doing or saying anything here James. You have caused this family enough trouble. I said I am not staying, I was only here for David and that he had no idea what he was talking about. None of them helped me when I was homeless. I gave Dave the keys to the car and called a very dear friend who owned a bar in Monroe and she came to get me. We went to her bar, I drank like a dysfunctional fish. Now it was a straight bar but when I went there everyone was very nice to me. Well the regulars, if someone had bad intentions, she or one of her friends would put them out. I, to this day, have huge respect and love for them. Huge hug to them all. Dave came later, he drove us home.

Chapter 16

So life is slowly getting back to normal. We see on the weather that a storm in brewing and her name is Katrina. I knew as she grew, there was no way we were going to ride it out so we made our plans to evacuate early on. Bought the stuff we needed and boarded up the condo and the shop. I get all of our insurance papers, important documents, cash and we are off. I was so happy we left two days early, we missed the traffic. I had one friend pass away on HWY 49. She was stuck in traffic, was so scared she had a heart attack. Love you Cindy! Despite of our due diligence, in the blink of an eye we lost everything! Katrina was the biggest insurance rip off of the century. Like the war GW dropped the ball. More on this later.

So David, Tash and I move back to Monroe. We start putting the pieces back together. This was not my first choice, but, David knew people here and so did I. I looked for a building to open a day spa and found one in West Monroe, on Antique Alley. Our insurance company denies all of our claims, we had coverage specifically for hurricane damage. So 23,000 people from the area file a class action law suit, we were two of them! I contacted the girls that worked with me in Biloxi, sent each of them 3,000 dollars to help them start over. I lease the building, have the inspection and it is not up to code. While I was having that taken care of, David and I paint, repair walls, work on floors and clean from top to bottom. It took 3 months and it looked wonderful. So Salon Style is ready for business. We had rented a townhouse not too far away and it was time to get busy. All money going out was not going to work for me. The salon was a duplex. On the smaller side we had 3 tanning beds, tanning products, clothing, jewelry, pageant supplies, statement pieces, crowns and shoes. Every style of shoe that I liked including one pair that came in my size! I loved going to market!! On the larger side I had 3 full stations. One for cutting and styling. One for color and a full makeup esthetician station and a full Mani Pedi set up. A private room for massage with a heated massage bed. Laser hair removal, waxing and a wet table for full body wraps and chemical peels. Believe me it was beautiful. Business picked up quickly and the shop was paying for itself within 3 months. David ran the tanning side, I the other. We settle in to a routine and try to get on with life. C.K. gets to visit, I could tell he was proud of us. The friend he had made in the service had been killed, I saw it weighed very heavy on his heart. He thought it was even friendly fire that killed him and that some Marine's knew about him being gay. I, for the first, time saw fear in his eyes. Because if they knew about that queer then they knew about him. I wanted to hide him away. A.W.O.L. He would not even consider it. He had to go fight with his buddies. The weekend he was with me he made out a will and we had it notarized. He told me some of the commanders had them torture people they had captured. He said to me, "I am now a monster." I told him he was not. The ones who placed the orders were. I held this man in my arms as he confessed the sins he was ordered to carry out. I was outraged! I assured him no matter what I loved him. I said when you go back, tell them you are gay, you can always work with me. Forget the discharge, he had a readymade family right here. I gave an oath to take care of him forever. He told me, baby you are the only reason I have to live. I didn't know what to say. His visit was way too short and I had not seen him in over a year. I drive him to Texas to catch his flight back to base. We still had to be careful. D.A.D.T. was in full force still and the debates all over the airwaves were heating up. In the fore front. John McCain. He is a war hero, but, no hero to me. If I would have known that was the last time I was going to see C.K., I would not have let him leave. As the plane flew away, I asked God to please protect him.

So some time passes. I had had a call from my man. He was safe and in a green zone. Oh what a relief. I had worried so about him. He had to go the phone card was empty. I immediately reloaded it with 500 dollars. Some two minute calls cost 50 dollars. The government sold the phone cards! I was having an amazing day in the shop and the phone rings. It was the attorney from the class action. He said we had an appointment with a federal judge and there was absolutely no way we could lose. We had been here a few years and to be honest I still hated the place!! I put the shop up for sale along with everything in it. Dirt cheap. It sold in a week. Our lease was up so I gave our notice we were going to move. I drive to see our cousins from mom's sister to look for a rental. We could catch up with them and the second move back to Biloxi would not be so far. David and I packed the U-Haul on the last day of our lease. I had bought a Red Mercedes SLK hard top convertible roadster. Gurl I was Ms. Fifi driving that machine, I loved it I knew C.K. would too. David had a white Isuzu Rodeo. We had found a house to rent and off we go. I am in the kitchen cooking, my phone rings, I don't recognize the number so I let it go to voicemail. Later I listen, it was a member of C.K.'s family asking me to please call them back. I call the number, terrified of what will come next. It was his brother. I had seen him in photos but we had never met. C.K. had been killed when his Humvee ran over an I.E.D. in Iraq. He said his death was instant and that he felt no pain. He needed my address to mail me a few things. I gave him the address, asked about the funeral. He said he would contact me when his body was back in the states. I thanked him for calling me. I put the phone on the counter top. Everything inside me had shut down. I had a pain inside of me that I would have done anything to get rid of. David comes running into the room. What's wrong little Bro? I told him. He goes to his room and cries. He had given his life for a country that didn't even want him to begin with. This was not how things were supposed to happen. This did not fit into my plan at all. I was completely devastated and mad as hell and every part of me wanted to die. Just like my friend so many years ago. I had David and Tash, the two main reasons for me to keep fighting. I went to my room and Tash crawled up next to me and laid her head on my arm. It was like she sensed he was gone. He had given her to me and she was such a comfort. From that day on she went everywhere I did. I was going through the actions of being alive. I was just empty inside. What was I going to do? God, what did I do to piss you off so bad? Only one thing took away the pain. Drinking and I did. A lot. I saw flashes of mom in me. I knew I did not want to be this person anymore. I still had some money in savings and that the class action would be over soon so we were going to be ok. I took my black suit to the cleaners, as to be ready for the funeral.

Two days after the call, a car turns into our driveway. Tash barked once, that was her way of saying, deal with it mom. I step onto the porch and this man walks up to the steps. Are you James Swift he asked? I answer yes sir, how may I help you. He hands me a large storage envelope. Then says you have been served. He turned, walked to his car then backs out and is gone. Served I thought? For what? I take my mystery package into the kitchen and sit at the island to open it. There was a letter in a white envelope and some papers from an attorney representing C.K.'s family. Legal terms I do not understand, if y'all saw the first draft of this book you would not I'm not big on spelling either. So I didn't know what those papers were for but I could read the letter. It was from his sister. As I read I learn the funeral is in 2 days and that I was forbidden to come. There was a restraining order placed against me. The family said I would be arrested on sight if I showed up. When will this nightmare ever end? He had not seen his family in DECADES!! All of my pain instantly morphed and became anger. I had to find out what the other papers meant. I called a client from the shop I worked at while living in the French Quarter. She was an attorney. I set up an appointment the day of the funeral. My mind was a blur and if I didn't know any better it felt as if everything in my heart was turning to stone. They had lied to me and as it turned out his body was already in the country. That meant he had been dead for weeks! Shame on them, shame on them all. His family wanted nothing to do with us because of their religious beliefs. I am so sick of that statement. I don't care if you are religious. Why use your church to hurt me? It was a 5 hour drive to New Orleans so I leave early. All I had to do was focus on driving and being safe. I knew what he and I had discussed I should do if he were killed. That was the hardest conversation of my life. Hopefully she was going to be able to tell me what to do and point me in the right direction. As I drive into the city, I see places we had gone together. Like the several times we had taken David to the Super Dome to watch the Saints play. I thought after I see the lawyer, I will stop and see some old friends. I park, go into the office and tell the receptionist my name. She will be right with you Mr. Swift, have a seat. Thank you I replied. It was probably a 10 minute wait but seemed like 10 hours. You can go in now Mr. Swift. As I walk into the office the first thing I notice is her hair. It looked awful! She said, LOOK AT MY HAIR!! It was a tad ash. Let's be honest, green was the color that came to mind. I will write down how her hair stylist can fix it for her, oh dear. I hand her what I have and as she reads her face is goes cold, almost like stone. She asks me, did he leave a will? I say yes as I hand it to her. She looks it over. Words come out of her mouth that I did not want to hear. This is not legal and it won't stand up in court. Court I ask? She then asks, did you have a palimony agreement? I had never heard those word's in my life, so the answer was of course no. She then said they are suing you for his belongings, savings, basically his part of everything. I ask her, almost not wanting to know, can they do that given that for years they were not involved in any part of his life? What she said next floored me. In the eyes of the law, you were only roommates. Roommates? I lost my breath. What do I do? She said hire a lawyer NOW!! She then gets on the phone. I write how her stylist could fix her hair on a notepad then mindlessly place it on her desk. She gave me a name and a number for a lawyer and says to call this man today. She had worked me in so there was someone waiting to see her. We hug and say goodbye. She asks me to please keep her posted. I didn't visit anyone that day and I drove straight home. The next few weeks were a nightmare! I called the lawyer and he took my case. I was also dealing with the other lawyer from Katrina. The love of my life was dead. I am understanding my mother's suicide more and more. This is still never going to be an option for me but I was able to shed a small ray of light on the subject. I had promised my brother I would not leave him ever again. David looked to me to make sure everything was going to be ok. I can say having him in my life is the only thing that has kept me going. When it became time for the rulings things went quick. I was called from the attorney in Biloxi. Remember he represents 23 thousand people. The judge had ruled and we were not getting a dime. The storm surge was said NOT to be a part of the hurricane itself, so the insurance company did not have to pay. That no one was covered. We needed a separate storm surge policy. If it had existed, I would have had it. The very definition of irony. According to the other lawyer I didn't have a leg to stand on. We could go to court and we would lose. Then I would owe tens of thousands in fees. So in just a few short years, everything I had worked so very hard for was gone. Went from being homeless, to being successful to… Everything ended up being for nothing. What was wrong with my country and its laws? Paying what I was ordered to pay bankrupted me. I had to sell my Mercedes, my furniture, my art, my appliances, even some of my hand made drag and wigs. Fifi didn't mind. We move in with the family friend who had told me about dad's bone cancer. Back in Monroe. This place just won't let me leave. Then my sweet little angel dog Tash had to be put to sleep. Dave and I cried for weeks. It turned out to be the very food I was feeding her that killed her. It was back when we had the bad dogfood from

China with all the chemicals in it. That made it even harder for me to bare. My life had completely fallen apart. Shortly after that my aunt lost her life to the brain tumors. I started to work in a shop that is in a major discount store nationwide. They took 60% of what I earned, that was if I made this enormous quota. If not they only paid minimum wage. A couple of years later my cousins in Mississippi, from my mom's side of the family, said, y'all come stay with us. David could live with one, me with the other. I buy a VW Cabrio Convertible and learned I could transfer to the same name shop in the retail store there. We moved. David would find scrap metal to sell, we both were working in chicken houses and I was working in the shop. Depression and drinking were my best friends. We had always loved mom's family. Still do to this day. As we were living there, I received a friend request from someone in West Monroe. We had a few mutual friends and some of the same interests. As we would post and message he started to follow what was happening as well as what had happened in my life and it turns out we had met when I was a kid. My mother used to do his Grandmothers hair. Later in life we were in the same horse riding club. I remember him riding, he was very good. His father had the same first and middle name as me. Months later he said I should come visit you. I told him I would have to ask my cousin and her husband because I was living with them. It was an overwhelming yes. So the visit was marked on the calendar. My cousin was so sweet to find out what he liked to eat. We cleaned as all southerners do before company comes. I was so excited. It had been almost 7 years since C.K. was killed. I needed that time as I didn't date at all. The day was here, Woo Hoo! My cousin's husband went to the tiny town that was nearby and he recognized the truck rolling into town from some pictures I had shown him. He motioned for him to follow back to the house being as if you didn't already know where their house was, you would never have found it. This was a good thing. My cousin had cooked all day. Suddenly, we see the two trucks driving up the hill. We go outside and he steps out of his truck. I will call him Boo as I did when I was on that show that I had been on. He is visibly nervous. We all hug, that is kind of my thing…Big Hug's y'all! Only once before in my life did I feel my heart beat like this when I first met someone. He was handsome, kind, polite, thin, but in a cowboy sort of way. I knew I could put some weight on him. After the ice is broken, things settle down quickly. This was to be just a weekend visit. We slept in separate room's thank you very much, I am not a HO! His visit was just to see if there were any sparks. Oh boy were there sparks. He just won everyone over right away. We hoped for another visit.

Chapter 17

I am not one to talk on the phone. I love to text, at least 3,000 a month to be exact. Boo was never into texting so when he got his first bill he had to change his plan. I blew up his phone. It wasn't a bad thing, we were just getting to know one another. He decides to come back and the energy between us was amazing. So on the second visit I get my first kiss. It was nice, very nice. I had forgotten how it felt to want to kiss someone. My fantastic family and brother were just as happy about him as I was. Things are looking up. Boo would bring Dave gifts and include him in things we would do. Just like C.K. did. My cousin and her husband went to visit his mother, they left Boo and me to talk. We discussed so much. I told him some of my past. Didn't want to scare him away with all of it just yet. He opened up to me as well. He had only came out to his parents the year before, was still in the closet for the most part. I knew how hard it was to be gay in that area, so I completely understood. With all the connections we had in life I felt like C.K. had sent him to me. Every time he would leave, we both would just cry. He would have to pull over after he drove away, just to get himself together and drive home. As the months pass he comes every other weekend and even spent his week of vacation with us. I was falling for this man. And I was scared to death. We had our first Christmas together and he finally said those 3 little words I hoped to hear. Got cab fare? I kid again. I love you. I was on top of the world. It is getting harder to say goodbye. A few visits later, we are in the living room, sitting on the sofa. He gets down on one knee and asks me to spend the rest of my life with him. Hands me a ring with a black diamond, he had one to match. I did not know this was coming, but, my cousin did. I don't know how she was able to keep that from me. I could not believe such a wonderful man loved me. I loved him completely. Someone loves me again, I hoped things were changing for me. They were just not as I had planned. The VW has engine trouble and dies forever.

As time passed my relationship with my cousin's husband was getting more and more stressed. I had gotten to the point that I didn't want to be in the same room as him. I decided to call a friend who lived nearby. I will call her Tink. Tink has been in my life for years. Truth be told she was the first and only girl I tried to date. She swears to this day the one kiss we did share is what turned me gay! I would come over to her house when I was in town visiting family to do her hair. She has two amazing boys and I just love them to death. Tink has not had the best of luck with men, but, through it all she is a survivor and an excellent mother to her children. I call and ask if it would be ok for me to stay with them awhile. She said yes in the blink of an eye. She was divorced at the time, so I would not be in the way. David also knows Tink and her sons. I am still just a couple of miles from Dave. I just walked away from my cousin's house. Did not tell her goodbye. I regret that now. But things between her husband and me had hit a boiling point. I was heartbroken for how it all worked out. She was the one who made me gumbo after mom died. To top it all off, she did everything she could to destroy me after I left. Even tried to get Boo to break up with me. I had never seen this mean side before. I never will again either. I have no trust in her at all, never will again. Once again someone who I loved and trusted turned their back. Tink picks me up while I am walking down the road. The next visit from Boo, he came to Tink's house. He meets them all and it is an instant like fest. Everyone approved. Now I was out of the stressful environment, but, it was getting harder and harder for Boo and I to say goodbye. I just love helping out around the house and the boys were now as tall if not taller than me. We had so much fun. Boo calls, he asked if I would consider moving back to Monroe so we could be closer together. He said if you find a job, I would help you find a reasonable apartment for you and David. I am a package deal, no matter what my brother has to be included. He knew that and it was no problem. I wasn't thrilled about coming back to Monroe again. But I loved this man. Being there with someone I cared about I figure it would be ok. I went online to see if the company I worked for had any openings in their salon. They did. Even better the Monroe store needed a manager. So I apply. The next day I get a call and am hired. This was on Wednesday, I was to have my first day of work and training the very next Monday. Small town is a very nice place to live. Just not for a Drag Queen. Fifi was starting to feel neglected. I would have to train for a few weeks in West Monroe with a coworker who was now the store manager. I call Boo, he was taken back by how fast it went, but, I could hear the excitement in his voice. I am very good with hair, he knew it. On his second visit I took over his, I had to. It was just not right. I called David, he was having issues with the other cousin as well. Mostly over me. So Tink and the boys say. Just have David come here until you get the apartment. I was so thankful they did. At first David was against it. He does not like change. Being with me and especially the last 8 years change had become common. I tell him that Boo and I would come get him and his things, he would get in the truck and it would be over with. The boy's just love David, he loves them too. And they all are so much fun to be around. He says yes, we get David settled that Saturday, so we can leave Sunday, for me to be at work Monday.

Everything between Boo and I just kept getting better and better. I had already met his parents, they were very nice. I had even started coloring his mom's hair. I would build up a clientele and Dave would work. Boo and I had discussed even living together in time. After C.K. I made a promise to myself that I would not put myself through all that goes with a separation if I was to fall in love again. I also made this fact very well known to Boo. So with complete honesty and no expectations we start this journey. Boo had found an affordable apartment the week before. It was near the Monroe store I was to be working in. He even furnished it for us. He is just too good to be true, so I thought. David and I did not have a car and it was only a 10 minute walk to the store. Now, where I was in relation to the train was many miles away. Boo was going to be taxi and when he couldn't I would take a real taxi. He didn't seem to mind. Everything was falling into place. So with me settled and the apartment ready we went to get David. We had a few things in a storage unit, so Boo hooked up his horse trailer to bring it back here. David and I now also had Jewel and Ruby. Our Cocker Spaniel and Pomeranian. About a year later we bred Ruby and that was how we ended up with Coco, her daughter. So here we are in this huge crew cab dually, pulling a horse trailer. We pick up our stuff, Dave and the two girls…Jewel and Ruby. On the way home we stop to eat. The girls were riding in the horse trailer. So the people got a laugh when we opened it to walk these two tiny dogs out of this giant trailer.

Right off the bat my skills were noticed. I was busy, the clients I had with my shop were coming as well. Word of mouth is the best though. Do something right and the ladies would spread the word like wildfire. Double edged sword too, because if you do something wrong, they tell twice as many people. I had started my management training while also working super hard to keep up with the clients. There were no appointments, walk in only. Time management was a nightmare. I specialize in cuts and color having extensive training in both. I kept up with all of the trends and new products. I also continued my education with at least 3 classes a year on advanced cutting and coloring techniques. The shop totals are going up and people are making more money and the manager was getting substantial bonuses. I am not sure where the mix up happened. I was almost finished with my training yet there was no mention of me leaving for the Monroe store. I had told my manager I was spending as much money as I was making on cabs to and from the West Monroe store. I was to be there three weeks and I was at this point going on three months. I emailed the district supervisor and asked when would I be transferred? She said we were under the impression you didn't want the manager's position. I never said that. I demand to be transferred so I was, but, not as the manager.

Dave had applied for work in the retail store the shop was in. He was hired and it felt great that we would be working inside the same building. I meet the ladies I will be working with and I like them all. One becomes a great friend. Once again the shop totals are going up. We were meeting our quota. I was using my knowledge of the computer when I looked up my time sheet. It was then that I saw some places in red. It appears that someone was shaving time off of me. I did not like this at all. The next week the District Supervisor came for a surprise visit. To see if she could catch us off guard I could guess. I could tell right away she did not like me. I was gay. She told me the manager's position was being held for someone with more experience! I have, at this time, been doing hair over 20 years and had been the owner of two very successful salons. I take her to the computer to show her where my time was being altered. She was surprised but because I was able to see it. I took notes honey whenever I was being trained. I make sure I learn. I knew it was time to start looking for another job. The manager's position was what I was hired for and I would not settle for less. About a week later I was in the mall. Boo had a birthday soon. The same hair company has several places located in the mall so I go to the one at the top. They charge more money and offer many more services. I ask the manager if he had any open chairs. He said not now but, would in the near future. I told him I already worked for the company. He said to go online and fill out an application for this branch. I did, he calls and I will have the next open chair. I call the District Supervisor and I give my 2 week notice and she fires me on the spot. I was packing up my stuff and had to call Boo so I could take it home. He was not happy with me even though I had another job lined up. I told him she fired me... I didn't quit. Made no difference now that he helped us financially as well, so I guess I didn't live up to what he thought he wanted. I didn't know it at the time but this was the moment that broke us. So once again I am the bad guy. It was going to be 4 weeks until I started in the mall. David was moved to full time and he was doing a great job. I'm so proud of him. Three weeks later Boo comes in and sits on the edge of the bed. He looks at me and says that he has met someone online and that they had hooked up. I asked if he wanted to see him again. He said I don't know. I sat there.... Boo had stopped coming by. He used to come on his lunch hour to let the girls out and walking them as David and I did not have time to. I only got 30 minutes for lunch. He also stopped texting except for what he had to. I had asked that he text me each day to be sure he made it home. My P.T.S.D. triggers and now I compelled to start worrying without a reason. He completely stops now. For his birthday, I buy a cake and a few gifts. Nothing fancy just stuff. Invited a couple friends over. He works 5 minutes from the apartment and gets off at 4pm. I tell everyone to go home when he is not there by 5:30 and throw everything in the trash by 6. I send him a picture of it all in the trash. He replied, oh my mom had something planned. I must have forgotten to tell you. I was furious! I had never been cheated on, I did not like this at all. I told him I have not even been here six months! Once again everything I had believed in had been ripped right out from under me. Before Boo met me he had guys on the internet he would hook up with. Most were married, had kids, which I am completely against. I could never do that to someone's wife. I kept telling myself this was his past. I was only interested in his future. David says I will support us little bro. That was so sweet. I told him I would be working soon as well. Looking back, I am ashamed of some of the texts I sent Boo in the heat of the moment. They were very mean. True, but mean. A few day's pass. Boo comes to the apartment. I am calling everyone I know to see about getting a ride to and from the mall as it was way too far to walk and I don't have the money for cabs. He wants to talk. He says everything right. I forgive him and we are back together. His parents offer to loan me the money to buy a used car. I had a friend here that owned a car lot. I had bought from him before, he was fair and I had no problems with any of the vehicles. I pick a red Solara Convertible. The parents say yes and we have a car payment now and insurance. Winter comes and I am so very happy David doesn't have to walk in the cold. Perfect arrangements as well with our schedules. David had switched to nights working the 10 pm to 7am shift and where I worked didn't even open until 10:00 in the morning.

So about a month goes by, Boo is spending the night. This is the night he asks me to help him with his phone. He never restarts it and never backs out of a browser or an app so I had to take the battery out to hard start the phone. It was rebooting and I said we need to delete your browser history. He said ok and to go ahead and do that. He is sitting right next to me mind you. During this process somehow his photos came up. Boom, nude pic of him. He didn't send it to me? So now I am getting that someone else must have gotten it. I scroll over a couple. Boom, nude pics of someone else. They were not together, it was like a sexting thing but I was pissed. I hand him his phone and when he looks it he starts to cry. He said I am not meeting them. He admitted he was searching the local Craigslist personals using the Grindr app. What concerned me was these people were local so they actually could meet. Then he says I don't have anyone to talk to about being gay. I said so you send them a picture of your dick? Like an icebreaker? He didn't think I was funny. I said why not talk to me? I can't talk to you about these things. Really? Boo Really? I tell you about my mother jerking me off and you have something more sensitive than that you need to talk about? I just get up and go to bed. The next morning he said he was sorry and that it would never happen again. That he loved me. That being in a relationship was new to him and that he was trying. I asked, did you have sex with him. He said no and that they had never met. I say ok, but, please talk to me. I am your partner. He says he will. I did not trust him so for now I stop all physical contact. I am HIV negative and I plan to stay that way. And yes I still love him. Boo start's drinking Vodka heavily every single time he spends the night now. I felt like he had to be drunk to even be around me. You will never know how bad that hurt me.

Chapter 18

Now I am working in the mall. The register is different and I have had no training on one like this. One particular coworker is so kind. She helps me with the register and becomes a dear friend. There were only two others at that time, the manager and another young lady. So a few months go by and I have an issue with the younger lady. While we are by ourselves during the shift she likes to throw around the "N" word. I do not approve of such ignorance. I felt I needed to bring this up to the manager. He brings us both to the stock room to confront the issue. She was very defensive but I did not hear that word from her again. So a few weeks later I notice that she starts refunding some money to my clients. Said I was over charging them. I didn't set the prices, the computer did. The real reason was we earned bonuses and points for being the top producer each month. She wanted to lower my totals. The manager did put a stop to that. But the damage was done. Word was spread I was an over charger. Then a few weeks later I noticed someone had been using my scissors. I keep them in a case and each one has its place. They are very expensive and I do not loan out my tools. The shop would supply everything except scissors. I had my own. I knew what each curling iron, flat iron, blow dryer and hot roller will do being as I owned my supplies not the shop. It was hands off. The next week my $150 steam flat iron was broken on my day off. Two weeks later my $200 dollar blow dryer was broken…again on my day off. Was I really going to have to carry everything home with me when I was not working to keep others from breaking them? What was this, grade school? I called the company, but, nothing is ever done about it. Randomly one day Boo and his parents call me and want to talk. They all come over and where our apartment was is in the middle of the biggest drug den here. I had no say in renting it nor have I once complained about living there. When Boo stopped coming around, we had to walk everywhere. Carry groceries, carry whatever we bought all the way home. I had to empty a can of mace on a man one night who started to chase me. I lost half of my food by the time I made it back to the apartment. They asked, if we buy a used trailer somewhere safe and made the payments the same as your rent would you like to do that? I told them I would have to talk to David and get back to them. We had had some shootings and drug busts at the apartment and the police were there every day. There had been a fire in one section and no one was hurt but they lost everything in the building. I talked to David, he leaves it up to me. I say ok. They pick me up the next afternoon and we drive a couple miles and end up near the local University U.L.M. and we turn into a trailer park to this lot I am in now. We walk through the trailer… it had good bones. I liked the floor plan. It has a master bedroom at each end. So David has a bathroom in his room and so do I. I just have a much bigger closet. Fifi takes some storage space. So as I said I liked it. It needed some paint and a TON of GAY style. I ask Boo to come outside with me. I say, if I do this, all of the online crap has to stop. You will have to start coming around more and we will go back to the way things were. He said that it would all be like it used to be and that he was 100% sure he loved me. I agree to the deal. Huge Mistake. At first it seemed like things may actually work out then he sets up a schedule for his visits. Every Tuesday and every other weekend. I was not happy with it but it was more than I was seeing him before. I paint and decorate then we all help in the move.

The shop in the mall is working my last nerve. I was to be off on Monday but I was called in. One of my clients happened to be buying some nail polish on Sunday. The young lady I had a few problems with was talking to her client and a few others when my client heard her say…and I quote. "I don't know why they hired James, you know he has A.I.D.S. don't you?" That was it. I called my friend, the other coworker and the manager. My client was not comfortable filling out a complaint form and I can't say I blamed her. I was beginning to think this person had some very serious issues. So I swallow my pride and put it behind me. Being so good with color, if there was a client done by a coworker that didn't like the result I was the one who was elected to redo it. This is how it works. I get the money from the original service plus any corrective techniques I had to use. I did three of these clients in one day. I missed all of the walk-in clients that day. Could not do my own clients that happened to stop by without an appointment either and I did two more the next week. I watched my totals, making a printout every day for 5 weeks. The money was never transferred to me. I was working for free. I had mentioned it to the manager, still nothing. $500 dollars may not be much money to some people, but it is to me. I didn't trust anyone except my friend in that shop. I quit, packed my stuff and left.

Boo said he understood why I left and that I would find another job. I was already looking. Boo and his parents had gone to Bonnie and Clyde days. It is a very big open air flea market. It only happens a few times a year. He comes for his Tuesday night sleep over and is showing me some photos he had taken. He scrolls one frame too far. Boom, naked man…again. He looked at me and started to cry. I sent him home. The next morning he comes over, sits on the bed. He said they hadn't met, that he was sorry and that he promised it would never happen again. I didn't know what to think. He was telling me he loved me but his actions told me something else. I don't like to give up on people. And I won't on someone I love that is until I see their actions are always going to hurt me.

I have a new job and the shop is right down the street. It is a booth- rent set up. There is a very professional staff and I try to put as much of my hair stuff in our car as I can. It was raining and my cart won't fit with the top up. Boo tells me he will swing by the trailer on his lunch hour then bring it to me. So that morning I am talking to everyone and all I have are the basics. I have my scissors and can do a cut and style but that is all. I even had a couple of walk-in customers. Noon comes around and we get a slight break in the rain. Boo called to say he was on his way and that he would be there in two minutes with my cart. Woo Hoo! I will have all I need for whatever walks through the door. Meanwhile we have one of our two shampoo bowls clogged. The maintenance person who worked for the owner stopped in to fix it. Just then Boo pulls up and I go help him with my cart. It is big and red. Actually it was really a tool box but it was just perfect for what I used it for. Together we bring it in. I introduce him to my coworkers who are there. The maintenance man comes around the corner. He sees my Boo and say's um, oh…hello. I look over at Boo and I kid you not, he turns white and returns the um, oh… hello in just the same awkward, peculiar way. He (Boo) then tells me he suddenly has to go. I thank him for bringing my stuff and to have a great day and off he goes. So I wheel my cart in place and open the drawers to fix anything that may have shifted in the move. My cell rings…its Boo. I answer and he tells me that he is still in the parking lot. Asks me to please come to his truck that he has something to tell me. I actually was confused but I tell him I will be right out. He was crying when I got into the truck. He said he needed to tell me before someone else did. I asked what? He said do you remember the last picture you saw in my phone of a dude? I said yes and he says, well that was him. Who was him I asked? The maintenance guy. I closed my eyes. I was getting tired of this little song and dance. He said there is more and I just looked at him. He went on to say we did sleep together. I didn't say a word. Just got out of the truck and went back in the shop. MY FIRST DAY!! I will be seeing this guy every time something needs fixing. I called Boo and I asked him did he (the maintenance man) know you had a partner. He said yes and that he does too. I hung up. Finished the day then went home. We are still trying to save our relationship. It is not looking good at all. A few weeks later I see this ad on television. It was going to be a new reality show on a major network. The announcer asked if you could change one thing about present day society what it would be. I thought EVERYTHING! The web site was given, so I sent an email. Just about what I would change and I threw in a few life experiences. I did get a reply the next day. It was how to audition and I needed to print out some pages to fill out. There was going to be a producer in New Orleans soon and they wanted me to make a video with some bullet answers from another page I printed. With them emailing me back, it kind of took my mind off what was going on. When I went to work the next day, I told my 2 favorite coworkers about it. They wished me luck. So a couple weeks go by. Dave and I just go to work, come home. I cook and clean and play with the three girls now. Boo comes when he wants to… which is not often. When he does either he was drunk by 7pm, or was taking some new sleeping pill from his doctor and drinking. He was all zoned out, looking crazy and drooling out of his mouth and trying to look around with one eye closed. I was furious but then he would want me to touch him. That shit was not gonna happen. If he was sober I may have but not like this. Oh how I was starting to hate my life. Now I knew for a fact he had cheated. Boo stops by one afternoon after work. It wasn't a scheduled visit so I wondered what was wrong. I am in my room and had just finished some laundry. We sit on the bed and he just starts talking. I don't love you the way you love me. I say really? He says I (meaning himself) was not ready for a relationship. I say we have been at it for two years and you are 50 years old and still living at home. When will you be ready Boo? The subject quickly changes when my phone rings and I can tell from the area code it was the people from the show. I go ahead and answer. I am invited to come to the New Orleans audition. Was not a public call. I had a time and date to be there. Boo says I can take you if you want to go so I tell the producer I will be there. Boo says how proud he was of me for having the courage to do this. I thank him and we continue to talk. Once again we are on the subject of money. How I just quit a job. He has no idea what it is like to be out and how people treat me. I didn't do any of the drag shows here because he didn't want to go. He did go out with Fifi but only two times. Then he said I tried it your way and I didn't like it. Two times. I didn't want to have a separate life from my partner. I told him all of this when we first met. I didn't want to be the couple who did everything apart. So I just stay at home. I was and still am so angry at myself. Why can't I stop giving a shit about this man? It is obvious he doesn't give one about me. Then he said, I thought I could handle the pressures of a relationship, family and work. I said we bought this trailer so you would stay more and you stay less. I am in debt up to my nipples to your parents because you said all the online crap would stop. I ask when were you going to move in and he said NEVER. I add we are already living separate lives and he agreed. I said, we are supposed to be your family now. He said, well you are not. That he had love for me but not romantic love. He knew that cut deep.

Wasn't a week later, he calls and he says he wants us to keep trying. I am an emotional wreck. My P.T.S.D. is getting worse. Now I have to switch gears. It was time to go to New Orleans and Boo drove us down. The people were very nice and I went into the interview alone. The questions stirred up some very old memories. I was told the process usually didn't take more than 20 minutes. They kept me 2 hours. When it was finished we drove home. Boo keeps calling to tell me that he misses me. He even let a couple I love you's slip. That gave me hope. I am getting regular emails from the casting agency. There was so much to do. And I learned how to make and send videos, along with photos. I was invited to Los Angeles for a screen test. To bring Fifi with me for some photo shoots and interviews. I am still working and trying to get all my stuff together. Didn't want to get there and have one boob, or 1 high heel. Boo is coming around more, so we patch things up. Everything seemed to be getting better. I fly to California where there is someone to meet me at baggage claim. Everyone was so kind. The hotel was fabulous! We were sequestered and that was a new word for me. We had so many appointments set up but we weren't supposed to see any of the other people who were there as well. I accidently was lead to an elevator before the doors closed and I saw Jeremy. I was scared of him at first but he turned out to be an incredible person. Soon enough my amazing trip was over. I fly home and Boo meets me at the airport. Things seem to be smoothing out and I am liking it. The next Saturday Tink comes to visit. She had not been here since we had moved back. Was so good to see her and to have someone to talk to that was straight from the hip. Tink don't play games. She will throw a man away and not look back if he wrongs her. We go to the shop so we could get her hair did! She tells me to follow my heart until I see there is nothing but pain coming my way. Then let the brain take over so I could heal. Made sense to me. It was a very good visit. The next weekend, once again I was working late on Saturday night. We have a local family here who has a reality show and the Father has some strong opinions about Gays. He had given one of his sermons on how evil we were, that we would not go to heaven. I wish these people would learn that there is a fringe of people who follow them that always acts on their words. I locked the shop door and was walking to my car. All of a sudden these two young white men shoved me into my car and held my arms and said "you had better watch your back faggot." Then they walked away. I was shaking and scared to death. I drove straight home. When David heard he wanted to go look for them but I would not let him. I went back Sunday morning and collected all of my stuff and left. I no longer felt safe and there was no way I was going back. The other guy that rented a booth where I had worked and his boyfriend worked in a hotel in West Monroe. I went in and filled out an application and was hired. I was to work in the kitchen, alone and serve the full breakfast they offered the guest's. Other duties were to clean the lobby and some first floor public bathrooms etc... I loved it. I learned quickly what I needed to do. I have always cooked and this was a very welcome change. Soon I was flying solo. Also two nights a week there was a managers special. We would serve beer, wine and some sort of finger food. Once I really got into the flow I took that over as well. I am super clean and extremely organized. I worked that kitchen into shape and cleaned out all the storage cabinets and the ovens. Also I was able to move the things that were stored in the house keeper's storage closets. Things are going great. The hours were not as convenient for David and me with one car. So we bought another. Red Beetle Convertible. Same colors as the Solara. Right down to the tan top. The show I auditioned for had already started and I was recording it and when I had time I was on the live feeds. That was where all the good drama happened. I loved the idea of what they were doing and the cast so far. I had pretty much given up on hearing from them ever again. So things between Boo and I were improving. I loved my job. Dave was in good spirits too.

Chapter 19

Boo was spending the night, we had just gotten into bed, when my cell rang. The area code was from the casting agency. I answered and it was like a conference call. Several of the producers were on the line. One asked me how things were. I said well, but, I was a little excited about them calling. Another said, James we would like to invite you to be on the show! I was elated. Started yelling and bouncing in the bed. I told Boo. He was so excited for me. So we end the call, I was going to get an email to tell me what to do. The welcome email came, I printed everything. I did not have long at all to get everything together and leave. Thinking about what someone would might need for a year is tough. Then add being a drag queen in the mix and I was going to have to get creative. A camera crew meets me at my trailer, we go all over the place, as well as here at home. It was a little awkward being in front of the camera. But I secretly loved it. I finally get packed, all my papers in order and it was the day to go to the airport. We take the Bug, Boo was going to wait with me until my flight boarded. We were in a good place and that made me very happy as I was setting out to change the world. Once again when I landed in California there was someone there to take me to a hotel. Oh my, the first one was nice. This one was amazing. I loved everything about it. They take my cell and wallet and the same drill as before. There were a few things to do as well. First was to pack all of my stuff I could fit into this little crate. That was not fun. I was not on speaking terms with that crate after half an hour. Then there was a team that had to check what we were taking and block out the labels. So I fast forward and I see who I am walking in with. It was the guy I saw in the elevator on the last trip. His beard was shorter but I was still uneasy about him. Turned out that I needed to learn a life lesson. I judged and I had judged wrong. He is a very good friend to this day along with his wife. Big hug's y'all. So we are in the compound. I just loved meeting everyone. But, as my life goes in 7 days the show was canceled. I can say it was the high point of my life to be accepted as a cast member. I didn't get a chance to talk much about my work with homeless GLBTQQ youth. I had planned to bring awareness to so many issues. It turned out the people who were watching on the internet embraced me and I have been able to get my message out and am working on opening the nation's first homeless as well as education shelter for these kids. The rollercoaster ride with Boo kept getting harder and harder to deal with. The constant switch from I love you to I don't love you and all the fear from the area I live in well...let's just say I finally broke. Mentally I hit rock bottom. I am hoping to be able to remain his friend, but, I don't know if I can. Once again I gave all to get nothing in return. I was abandoned once again by the very one I trusted and loved the most. I will not give up on me, David nor Fifi. World... you have not heard the last from any of us. I will move forward and I will live in pure joy once again. If someone out there needs a hug, I am sending it. If you need a friend, here I am. We all have to share this planet together. I, for one, look forward to meeting as many new faces as possible. LOVE TO YOU ALL!! Ok let's get back to the story. Next, you will read about the first homeless kid I ever helped.

One event in New Orleans I have always loved is Mardi Gras and we always had standing room only for the shows. Everyone was just happy to be there and it showed. On lundi Gras we would start the shows at noon and work all the way through to 11pm on Fat Tuesday only stopping to eat, use the restroom, or shave and reapply our makeup. The tips were amazing. Some days up to 900 dollars. There are just so many people. Midnight signals the start of Ash Wednesday, the police and National Guard close the streets. Time for a massive cleanup. The shop was open for business, sometimes I did my clients as Fifi, they didn't mind. In fact some preferred it. She is a ham.

One show I will always remember. I had decided to do all Patsy Cline songs. I sang live and I am proud of my Patsy drag. I had all of my wigs backstage and my different jewels were all out and organized. I was told if I was any more anal retentive that the chair I sat on would disappear. It was my O.C.D., well it was C.D.O. to me because of course it had to be in alphabetical order. The audience went wild as I stepped out to do "Crazy". I was sporting a 50's style dress. It was black and trimmed in black feathers. We always closed the show with a number from the Best Little Whore House in Texas. All the cast and special guests were in the final production number.

My best friend D.D. would be the Madame and point to each girl for their line in the song. It was great fun, upbeat, left the crowd in a good mood. After the show we would meet backstage and change into our travel drag and make the circuit. Bourbon St. was always packed with locals and tourist alike. We loved for the tourist to stop us and want to pose for photos with us. I always said Fifi went home with more tourist in their cameras than the hookers did. We arrive at the club where the exotic male dancers perform. It was packed, but a pack of drag queens can part a crowd like the Red Sea. There was this kid inside the club that caught my eye. Obviously too young to be out at this hour and probably to be in the club at all. I asked him to sit with me for a chat and bought him a coke. His clothes were dirty. His breath was really bad, so I knew he wasn't brushing his teeth regularly. I learn he is 17 and had been on the streets for two years. This broke my heart. I knew what he was doing to survive… hustling. Selling his body as I had done it myself at that age. He had a very bad cough and was so thin and frail. I called David on his cell and asked if he would mind if I brought this young man home for some food, a shower and a good night's sleep. David is just as much a softie as I am. He said no problem. We hopped in a cab and off we go. Earlier I had fried some pork chops, mashed potatoes, gravy and had made a mixed green salad. In my mind there is nothing more satisfying than a good ole home cooked meal to make someone feel better. I wondered when was the last time this poor kid had something to eat. I fixed him a plate and warmed it in the microwave. David poured him a big glass of sweet tea. As he ate I got a new toothbrush for him and picked out some clean clothes to put on after he showered. I jumped in the shower to wash off my makeup and become James. We had a stacked washer and dryer and I was going to see if Tide could help his clothes not stand on their own. I give him a washcloth and a towel then show him where the toothpaste was along with the mouthwash. I told him to put his clothes in the basket and I would wash them when he was finished. When he closed the bathroom door, I heard it lock. This kid has been abused I thought to myself. I could hear him coughing in the shower and I hoped the steam was doing him some good. When he is finished he brings me the clothes basket and said that was the best shower ever. We get him settled on the sofa then we talk some more. He said Ms. Fifi was very pretty and I told him thank you. He was not from Louisiana. He had hitch hiked from Texas. His father was a minister in a full gospel church. He caught this child fooling around with another boy at church camp. He was beaten severely. When he saw the chance, he ran away. He thanked me again for feeding him and for letting him stay the night. I told him it was our pleasure. I carry the basket to the washer and put in the clothes, detergent and started it. As I was walking out of the little nook where the machine was I saw he had taken the shorts off and uncovered himself and was naked. My heart sank. He thought that was why I was being nice to him. I said oh no that is not why you are here and to please put the shorts back on. He looked puzzled but he did as I asked. He went on to say that it seems the only time someone is nice to me is when they want sex from me. I was so very worried about his cough as it was deep and had a rattle. I told him not in this apartment that he was our guest. I didn't have anything pressing until 6pm the next day so in the morning I was going to take him to the charity hospital. I could be his cousin if they asked. So when he is seen by the doctor there are tests ordered and chest x-rays. A few of the tests would not be ready today and I needed to bring him back for the results when they called. I was told to buy some children's cough syrup and to make sure he drinks plenty of water. He stayed with us until the tests were in. Dave was home full time now so I wasn't worried about anything being stolen. We go back for the test results… this 17 year old child had AIDS. Not HIV but full blown AIDS. Back then this was a diagnosis of death. Then this young man said something that shook me to the bone. He said I got it on purpose. I had unprotected sex with men who had AIDS so I would be able to live in a shelter. To get off the streets. He said they were called bug chasers and the men were known as bug givers. I had never heard of this and was sick to my stomach thinking about it. I was angry at his parents and I was angry at these bug giver people. I was going to find them and put a stop to it and I DID! He started his treatments a few days later and it was not long at all I was able to get him in a medical shelter. I would visit every other day. A very few short months later this sweet gentle child died. I knew then I had to do something for these kids. I remember seeing so many asking for change on the street. We would just walk past them. To this day I will see a kid that reminds me of him with scruffy brown hair and I shed a tear. This was the first of many that would stay with us in transition to a shelter. We were not the only ones doing this. Many in the LGBTQQ community were. I figured with my contacts I had made from doing shows all over this country that we could form a safety net for these kids. At least get them off the streets a night. Feed them. Sadly, like in any community, there are those who would exploit these kids and take advantage of the situation. Not in my home and not in my heart. We all need to show more love, compassion and especially understanding. The hate is far too real. Many say you are breaking the law helping these kids. Well their families broke a human law by casting away their very own. All I am trying to do is help. My lifelong dream is to open a learning and teaching shelter for these kids. Get them off of the streets and help them earn a GED or teach them a trade so they will be able to take care of themselves and live a productive life. Keep a look out for L.T.A - Life Training Academy. I have already started the legal work and fundraising. I will make this happen!

Chapter 20

I now want to take you on a journey to Casper Wyoming. I was watching the news while working in the shop. There was a story of a young man who was tied to a fence, beaten and left to die. The reporter said it was suspected this happened to him because he was gay. My heart sank. I had survived my attacks and knew this could have just as easily have been me. I called around, everyone was talking about this. We were concerned for his wellbeing and for all like us in his area. Add to that mad as hell! The hospital had someone that would read updates on his condition. We now know his name Matthew Shepard. I knew I had to go, we all wanted him to pull through. He didn't. It was October, I packed the car for my road trip. Dave was there to see me off. As I drove away I had a very heavy heart. I kept having flashbacks of my attacks all the hateful people I had endured through the years. From Christian radio, televangelist, politicians and the good ole boy home grown terrorist's that were in every single state. What lead up to us being targeted for such horrible crimes? The right winger's spewing their hate of no special rights. No one was asking for special rights, just equal rights. C.K. dying in the closet, I spent thousands of dollars on medical bills, injuries given to me by my fellow Americans. I was furious at my countrymen, my government and most of all God. How could he exist and allow people to act this way in his name? I knew they were going to use the gay panic defense when these two boys went to trial. I arrive in Casper October 17th. Such a beautiful place. As I drive I see signs wishing Matthew well, as I walk I hear the chatter from people who say I can't believe it happened here. I could. I asked a few people where this had happened, I was given directions. I had flowers from friends to place there. There was sadness in the air, knowing not that long ago a person was fighting for his very life in this space. The temperature was crisp, there was a mix of sleet and snow. Some of the police tape was still tied to the post. Many people had brought flowers, candles, stuffed animals, cards and photos of him as well. I placed our flowers in a good spot. Then turned to look at the countryside towards town. I could not hold back my emotions and started to cry. To be in that spot, clinging to life by a thread, at no fault of his own broke my heart. To this day I wonder why I survived two attacks. If it happened again would I survive? How long would it be before someone killed me? I think every single day as I walk out of my home…Is today the day? I could not find a motel room. Everything was full of media folk and likeminded people as me who wanted this to be an eye opener for our country. To see how their perception of us effected our daily lives. I park as close to downtown as I can. As I walk, looking for a place to get something to eat, I wonder how many times my dead brother in life walked this path? I find a diner go in and then find a seat. It is pretty busy and I see reporters, camera and sound people with their equipment. So many I could tell were LGBTQQ. I order my meal and I over hear some talking two booths to my right about the funeral services and how they were going to respond with this church that was going to picket it. I had not heard of this church. I ask may I listen in and that I had driven in from New Orleans to pay my respects to Matthew, his family and the community. They squeeze me into a booth and they start telling me of this man and his church of hate. I could not believe my ears. He protested gay funerals and his church made up of mostly family. Then showed me photos of some of their signs. I was going to see this person the very next day. One asked where was I staying? I said in my car because there were no rooms. She said you can bunk with me, there is an empty spot on my floor. I said only if you let me pay some on the bill. She agreed so we eat and have some coffee. I hear how they travel all around the country trying to expose these stories of how LGBTQQ people are treated. They tell me of so many attacks and murders. How some live in total fear. I understand this more now than ever. As we talked I wondered if this funeral was going to turn violent. My new roomie and I get ready for bed. I tell her of my life, about C.K. and my attacks. She suggested I write a book. I laughed…who would read it? It would be all about the freaks and social misfits. She said you mean dykes and queers? I answered yes. We exchanged email addresses and I still get an email from her time to time. I now can see the changes in our country for people like me. With so much fighting and legal battles it takes a toll on us. Arriving at the funeral a light snow was falling. I could see the church family across the street with those horrible signs. Some were children. I was disgusted. I was shocked at the language being used by them as well. The police were protecting the protesters who were behind make shift plastic barricades. Back and forth the insults flew becoming viler by the minute. Someone behind the barricade said you will burn in hell you filthy faggot and as I turned I saw he was looking at me. I felt like the air around me weighed a ton and I could not breathe any of it in. I thought about David and what would happen to him if I was killed here. I say my goodbye's then go to my car. I was so angry but my fear was much greater. I regret leaving, given my past I had no choice. I was on auto pilot all the way home. I knew things for people like me would continue to get worse.

I am home now from my time on the show and I made many friends while in California. I cherish them all. I was posting every step I was making online not thinking of any repercussions. I was going to drive to New Orleans to meet a fellow cast mate. Have a few drinks and laugh a little. I had an amazing time and met some really cool people. Some had even watched the live feeds. Fifi was wearing a black body suit, royal blue knee boots with ruffles and 4 inch heels and a royal blue sheer jacket. Multi colored rhinestone jewelry. The next day I drive home and I posted I was going to fill up the car with gas then go make groceries. Yes, in Louisiana we make groceries. I was at the filling station just about finished at the pump. Someone says Hey Fifi. I smile and look up just in time for an unopened can of soda to hit me right in my face. They sped off in an older model Toyota pickup. There were no cameras and no one saw the people's faces nor the license plate. My nose was broken and I looked like hell therefore Fifi was not going to be seen for quite a while. My PTSD went into overdrive to the point of not wanting to leave my home. The next ordeal was when I had let girls out to do their business in our fenced yard and I saw something inside the fence and I didn't know what it was. I closed the gate from the porch to the yard so the girls would have to stay on the porch. It was a piece of fried chicken with rat poison all over it. To this day when we let them out we check the yard first. I was having trouble before I even went to California with some of my neighbors. I don't bother anyone so why bother me? They damaged our trailer and both of our cars. Finally they were evicted.

All of my life I have had firsthand experience with the hate and bigotry in America. Being treated like a second class citizen. Daily having to hear that there is something wrong with me. Either in person, in the media or church. I have spent my entire life standing up for myself and people like me. Even those who are not like me. Being on the front lines for so many years I have the scars all over my body from ignorant home grown terrorist's cloaked in the cape of organized religion or government. My PTSD is to the point my hands shake so bad I can't do hair anymore. My career may be over. In my area I fear others every day. I am just as much of an American as any other born in this country so why am I treated so differently? Because of a book I don't even know if I believe in anymore? I have had to conform every single day of my 48 years thus far to other's laws, beliefs and prejudices.

I have the most amazing online family in the world. They have gotten me through so much. I thank you all. I will never have a fan I will always have family. I have always wanted to walk my path with understanding, love and compassion. I do believe in the do unto others rule. In my life it is becoming harder and harder to find this compassion.

I would like to thank you for reading my book and I ask that you step out of your comfort zone and try to see we...the people. It's not this or that group. It is every single one of us! I do not want pity nor sorrow. I own my gayness along with all my actions in life. I hope someone will find understanding in my words. It truly takes us all to bring change and to make it work.

Big hug's y'all

Fifi Frost

L.T.A. Mission Statement

Life Training Academy

At L.T.A. it is our utmost and heartfelt mission to extend a loving, supportive and protective much needed hand to the LGBTQQ who have been carelessly thrown and cast aside, by those who were supposed to love and care for them. To remove these amazing children from the cold and calloused streets from which they were forced to live on. To provide food, clean clothes and a bed at a safe and loving shelter. At L.T.A. we strive to provide more than just shelter. By partnering with national and local businesses to teach employable skills, offering GED courses with the additional help of local tutors. Our dream is to walk hand in hand with these kids, guide, direct and encourage them to begin the process of healing. By addressing rejection, sexual abuse, physical abuse, family and social phobias and hurt. To toil through these monumental challenges and help sculpt strong, independent, proud, productive members of society. So they have the tools and skills to live up to their God given potential and become mentors of hope themselves. This has been a lifelong dream of mine and I WILL see it happen. I all too well know the trials and unjust tribulations that these incredible kids have to endure. I know what it takes to survive on the streets after being discarded myself at the age of 15 and it has to end.

Made in the USA
Monee, IL
14 June 2020